STEM
Education Reform
in Urban
High Schools

STEM
Education Reform in Urban High Schools

Opportunities, Constraints, Culture, and Outcomes

MARGARET EISENHART
AND LOIS WEIS

Harvard Education Press
Cambridge, MA

Paperback ISBN 978-1-68253-762-6

Library of Congress Cataloging-in-Publication Data is on file.

Published by Harvard Education Press,
an imprint of the Harvard Education Publishing Group
Harvard Education Press
8 Story Street
Cambridge, MA 02138

Cover Design: Ciano Design
Cover Image: iStock.com/da-kuk

The typefaces in this book are ITC Stone Serif and ITC Stone Sans

*We dedicate this book to the students
who participated in this study,
their families, and others like them.*

CONTENTS

CHAPTER 1 Education Reform for a STEM-Centered Future   1

CHAPTER 2 Launching STEM Education Reform in Denver and Buffalo   17

CHAPTER 3 Erosion of STEM Opportunities, Especially in Buffalo   33

CHAPTER 4 Diverting and Outsourcing College and STEM Counseling   53

CHAPTER 5 Figured Worlds of Success in High School Math and Science   77

CHAPTER 6 Educational and Occupational Outcomes   99

CHAPTER 7 A Closer Look at STEM Trajectories in Denver   129

CHAPTER 8 Minding the Gaps   157

APPENDIX Research Methodology   171

Notes   185
Acknowledgments   203
About the Authors   207
Index   211

CHAPTER 1

Education Reform for a STEM-Centered Future

"The rhetoric about science, technology, engineering, and mathematics (STEM) education in urban schools reflects a desire to imagine a new city that is poised to compete in a STEM-centered future. Therefore, STEM has been positioned as a critical part of urban education efforts."[1]

Reform of science, technology, engineering, and mathematics (STEM) education has been a persistent concern in the United States for decades. People educated in STEM are considered increasingly important in preparing for a future of innovation, advancing knowledge, and improved societal well-being. In recent years, strong education in STEM has been promoted as especially important for groups historically underrepresented in the expanding and future-oriented STEM-related fields. These groups include low-income students, Black and Latino/a minoritized students, and girls and women.[2] Recent national data suggest strong interest in STEM among these youth, yet the number of young people from underrepresented groups who attain STEM degrees or pursue STEM careers remains small.[3] In this book, we tell the story of STEM education reform efforts in eight predominantly minority-serving high schools in two cities: Denver, Colorado, and Buffalo, New York (four schools in each city). The schools were generally representative of urban, public, nonselective, non-charter high schools where efforts to broaden participation in STEM are currently underway, and the students we studied at these schools were generally representative of the type of student who is the focus of contemporary efforts to broaden participation in STEM.

A variety of high school models for improving STEM education have been proposed in recent years. They range from highly selective high schools—created for top-performing students with the highest grades and test scores in math and science—to "inclusive STEM-focused schools" with no admission requirements and an explicit goal to serve historically underrepresented students.[4]

Today's inclusive STEM schools are extremely varied. Some are almost entirely devoted to STEM; some have STEM tracks within larger comprehensive schools; some are traditional public schools, others are charters; some are small, others are large; some serve well-resourced students, others do not. And the number of these schools and programs is increasing every year, as more and more states and school districts are experimenting with inclusive STEM schools and programs.[5]

Despite the increasing popularity of inclusive STEM schools, research on them is limited, and the existing research has been primarily descriptive—documenting the characteristics of students who attend STEM schools and the curriculum goals and planned enhancements at these schools.[6] Where outcome data exist, they are decidedly mixed.[7] Some studies suggest that, when compared to students in traditional comprehensive high schools, students in STEM schools take more advanced math and science, express more interest in STEM careers, and are more likely to enroll in STEM college majors. Some research suggests that historically underrepresented and female students appear to do especially well in these schools. Other studies find that there are no effects on standardized test scores or STEM outcomes for underrepresented groups and that gender and racial gaps remain the same or widen, with girls and students of color falling behind.

The popularity of inclusive STEM schools and the disparate findings make clear that more research is needed to better understand these schools and the outcomes they produce. We need to know what goes on in these schools. We need to know whether differences in outcomes exist, and if so, why. We need to know whether these schools are preparing students for a future in STEM. To address these needs, it is essential to have details about the curricula of specific schools, the implementation of their programs, the nature of their student populations, and the outcomes they achieve with respect to broadening participation in STEM. The study described in this book was designed to contribute to this understanding.

STEM EDUCATION REFORM IN DENVER AND BUFFALO

Beginning in the late 2000s, school districts in Denver and Buffalo made ambitious plans for inclusive STEM education reform. Unlike in some places where state officials have directed and monitored STEM reform, the efforts in Denver and Buffalo were initiated and developed in local districts by administrators, school leaders, and community members. Teachers, parents, and students expressed excitement and interest in the possibilities of STEM schools. Some inclusive STEM-focused high schools were opened in each city.[8] At the same time, some traditional comprehensive high schools increased their STEM and advanced STEM offerings in line with general proposals for STEM education reform.

In 2009, there was one STEM-focused public charter school operating in Denver, the (Stapleton) Denver School of Science and Technology (DSST). There were no test-in, selective, or private STEM schools in Denver. Similarly, Buffalo had one STEM-focused public school prior to 2009, Hutchinson Technical High School, which was a test-in school. There were no private STEM schools in Buffalo prior to 2009.

In 2009, we set out to investigate and compare STEM education reform programs and outcomes in two inclusive STEM-focused high schools and two traditional high schools in each city. All the schools were public (non-charter) high schools with open (nonselective) admissions policies. At each of the eight high schools, we examined STEM course organization and offerings, teacher qualifications, classroom activities, student experiences, and counseling. All teachers of STEM subjects in the schools were full-time teachers who were certified to teach in their respective areas. At each school, we focused our attention on the opportunities and experiences of ten to twelve "focal" students who were in the top 20 percent of their high school class in math and science, based on ninth-grade standardized test scores, grades, and teacher confirmations. Among this group, we over-selected for minoritized students.[9] (See the appendix for details of site selection and data collection.) We used these criteria because we wanted to focus on the experiences of "high-achieving" minoritized students who were likely to be eligible for and interested in the highest-level math or science opportunities at their respective schools. From 2010 to 2013, we conducted interviews with students, teachers, counselors, administrators, and parents at each school. We also observed in classes and school common areas. We collected various school documents including policy statements, curricular offerings, and official student transcripts. In 2015 and again from 2017 through 2019, we added follow-up surveys and interviews with these focal students to learn what they did after high school.

When our study began (2010), the public schools in Denver had a majority Latino/a population, mostly Mexican American, with 74 percent of all students eligible for free or reduced lunch (FRL). The public schools in Buffalo had a majority Black population, with 77 percent eligible for FRL. At that time, both cities were projected to have expanding scientific and technology sectors with employee shortages in the near future.[10] In spite of different economic bases, social mobility rates were similar in the two cities.[11]

Denver: The City and Its Schools

At the time our study began, Denver was known as a relatively vibrant and growing city but was plagued by segregation (Mexican/Black/White) and pockets of high poverty. During the decade before our study began, there had been consistent support for STEM reform in the city's multiple school districts. Ideas related to STEM reform included curricular upgrades, new buildings, and technological innovations. Schools in all city districts had experienced some support for these improvements, even in the challenging economic times of the 2008 recession.

The high schools in our study were located in the three Denver metropolitan-area school districts with the highest representation of minoritized students. The schools were Chavez, Pella, Southside, and Capital. (All school names in both Denver and Buffalo are pseudonyms.) All four schools were large, with student populations of approximately 1,750 at Chavez and Southside and 2,300 at Pella and Capital.

The two STEM-focused schools in Denver were Chavez and Pella. In 2010, both were housed in brand-new buildings and organized as non-selective (inclusive) academy schools—with students divided into academies including at least one focused on STEM. In principle, academies bring students with similar career interests together for more focused and specialized instruction in hopes of improving educational as well as career outcomes; such schools are sometimes referred to as "career academies."[12]

Chavez had the Science and Technology Academy. Pella had the Engineering Academy and the Health/Medicine Academy. At both schools, a set of core-subject teachers (math, science, English, social studies) was assigned to each academy along with teachers for that academy's specialized courses. The academy's core-subject teachers were responsible for orienting their traditional coursework to the academy theme. Each incoming student was asked to self-select an academy before enrolling at the school. The administration's expectation was that a student would stay in the chosen academy for the duration of their time at the school. The program was intended to enable students to take at least one course per semester in each core area and one academy-specific elective—for example, Robotics, Principles of Engineering, or Health Trends—and thereby to prepare them well for postsecondary or career options in the areas of the chosen academy.

Both Chavez and Pella had functioned in old buildings as traditional comprehensive high schools for many years prior to their reorganization as academy schools. With the reorganization, both schools were replaced by beautiful new buildings with modern facilities. As the two new schools prepared to open, they prominently advertised their new facilities and new academy structure, particularly the STEM-focused academies, on their websites, in interviews with news outlets, and in written materials mailed to parents in the Denver metro area. Both schools began their first year as academy schools with uncharacteristically positive press coverage and larger-than-expected enrollments.

In initial interviews, the school principals at Chavez and Pella were very enthusiastic about the promise of the academy schools. They were eager to begin the school year in their new buildings. They were energized by the new structure that would group students around a career theme with a designated group of teachers. They looked forward to attracting neighborhood students who had open-enrolled elsewhere as well as students living outside the district who would be attracted to the academy structure.[13] Unstated in these interviews was the fact that both schools were operating under school improvement plans required by the state for previous failure to meet federal achievement goals.[14] The new buildings and programs brought uncharacteristically positive press and new energy to both schools.

The two other schools in Denver, Southside and Capital, were large comprehensive high schools that had been organized in traditional ways for many years. In recent years, both had experienced significant increases in enrollment from students who open-enrolled from outside their neighborhood boundaries (suggesting that parents and students found Southside and Capital more desirable than their neighborhood schools). Like Chavez and Pella, Southside was operating under a mandated school improvement plan for failing to meet federal accountability requirements; Capital was not.[15]

Table 1.1 shows the demographic characteristics of the four schools in Denver (Chavez, Pella, Southside, and Capital) and the demographic characteristics of the focal students at each school in 2010 when our study began.

Buffalo: The City and Its Schools

In contrast to Denver, Buffalo was known as a poor, shrinking, highly segregated, and largely Black/White city with a history of failing schools. Buffalo was also increasingly home to an influx of newcomers, with a large population of refugees, including people of Burmese, Bhutanese, Somali, and Iraqi descent. When our study began, there was some evidence that the economic situation was turning around on account of large infusions of capital from the state and the development of a downtown medical corridor. In Buffalo, public support for schools was less generous than in Denver, but district efforts were underway to improve the schools and STEM education in particular. An op-ed piece in the local newspaper mentioned the creation of STEM programs

TABLE 1.1 *Focal student and school demographics, Denver**

	CHAVEZ (STEM FOCUSED)		PELLA (STEM FOCUSED)		SOUTHSIDE (COMPREHENSIVE)		CAPITAL (COMPREHENSIVE)	
	Focal	School	Focal	School	Focal	School	Focal	School
% Free or reduced lunch	84.6	74	33	74	100	93	8.3	64
% Race/ethnicity								
Asian	0	0.4	33.3	7.3	10	2.9	16.7	2.1
Black	0	3.4	8.3	2.1	0	1	25	17.5
White	15.4	14	33.3	24.1	0	3.2	16.7	44.1
Latino/a	69.2	81	25	64.7	90	91.7	16.7	21.5
Multiracial/ other	15.4	0.2	0	0.9	0	1.2	25	5.2
% Gender								
Male	30.8	52	50	51	63.6	54	41.7	48
Female	69	48	50	48	36	46	58.3	51

*Figures for focal students were compiled by us; figures for schools were provided by the school district. In some cases, categories do not total 100% due to rounding.

in Buffalo and declared, "The school system can be a magnet to draw people back to the city and reverse urban decline."[16] While there was some community skepticism about the district's ability to successfully implement STEM reforms, the news outlets commended the creation of these new programs, and the newly envisioned STEM schools were eagerly anticipated.

The two STEM-focused schools in Buffalo were STEM Academy and Broadway Science. Both were designated "STEM schools" by the school district and were represented as such by the school superintendent. In 2006, STEM Academy was introduced as a stand-alone inclusive STEM alternative to other district options, enrolling students in grades 5 through 12. As part of the mandated school improvement plan required by the state for failure to meet federal achievement goals, what had been a failing vocational school was reopened under a new name and scope as STEM Academy. STEM Academy had moved to a new temporary home just prior to our study, and then to a newly constructed building during the summer before the final year of our study.

STEM Academy was created under a three-year contract with College Board, which sent support in the form of curriculum and professional development.[17] A key component of the College Board model was accelerating students in math and science to take Algebra and Biology (typically ninth-grade courses) and US History (typically an eleventh-grade course) in grade 8 so that they could take Advanced Placement (AP) STEM and other AP courses in tenth and eleventh grades. District administrators hoped these changes would facilitate high-level STEM in college and career for low-income students, particularly low-income and minoritized students of color.

The second district-designated STEM school in Buffalo, Broadway Science, was reopened in the 2005–06 academic year (replacing another failing high school) as a comprehensive high school with a specialized STEM program, the Biopharmacy program.[18] The new school recruited students by contacting parents of middle school students with high grades in math and science and offering the students the opportunity to attend the school and participate in a specialized science program. The Biopharmacy program was intended to be a high-level, academic STEM option for low-income underrepresented students of color, and was created in partnership with a local Research 1 university. Its stated purpose was to prepare students for higher education leading to high-level jobs, particularly in research. The school also offered a nursing program—officially known as the "HOT program" (Health Occupations Technology); students in this track were prepared to become certified nurse assistants (CNAs). The HOT program was conducted in collaboration with a nursing program at a local college. Students in the HOT program had to meet the basic New York State requirements for graduation, take an Anatomy and Physiology course, and complete a clinical placement. In addition, a Forensics program was added to Broadway Science a year after the Biopharmacy program began. This program was originally envisioned as a second high-level science-based program with a similar structure as Biopharmacy, but the district decided to open the program in a Career and Technical Education (CTE) track instead.

The other two schools in Buffalo—Lincoln and Global Horizons—had also been recently restructured for failing to meet federal standards.

Lincoln hired a new principal with a mandate to produce higher test scores and graduation rates. Global Horizons, created after the dissolution of a large, comprehensive high school that was struggling, was similar to STEM Academy. Global Horizons followed a small-school model and opened with College Board support. Unlike STEM Academy, however, Global Horizons was established as a comprehensive high school. Both Global Horizons and Lincoln opened with plans to markedly intensify their STEM-related course offerings.

As in Denver, there was tremendous public enthusiasm for these new school openings, and parents and students were excited to pursue promised high-level STEM offerings leading to college and career opportunities in both STEM-focused schools and traditional comprehensives that pledged to markedly improve offerings in math and science. Hopes ran high among parents and students in the district, and the schools, like those in Denver, quickly filled to capacity.

Table 1.2 shows the demographic characteristics of the four Buffalo schools and the focal students at each school.

Focusing on "High-Achieving" Students

In designing our study, we made the decision to focus on *high-achieving students* at each school. We defined *high-achieving* for the purposes of our study as students who scored in the top 20 percent of their high school class on achievement tests in math and science at the end of grade 9. We expected these students to be the most likely to have access to and take advantage of the most challenging courses and other STEM-related experiences at their school. We also judged them to be best positioned to consider STEM postsecondary education and career opportunities. To be clear, each sample of high achievers was *relative to their school*. Our interest was in the "best-case scenario" with regard to opportunities and outcomes for STEM in nonselective urban high schools that serve low-income and minoritized students.

Comparing Students and Contexts

As can be seen in comparing tables 1.1 (Denver) and 1.2 (Buffalo), we could not precisely match schools and students within or across cities.

TABLE 1.2 *Focal student and school demographics, Buffalo**

	BROADWAY SCIENCE ACADEMY (STEM FOCUSED)		STEM ACADEMY (STEM FOCUSED)		GLOBAL HORIZONS (COMPREHENSIVE)		LINCOLN (COMPREHENSIVE)	
	Focal	School	Focal	School	Focal	School	Focal	School
% Free or reduced lunch	100	77	54	80	100	86	73	77
% Race/ethnicity								
Asian	0	0	0	1	38.9	8	9.1	1
Black	87.5	94	53.8	84	27.8	55	72.7	87
White	0	3	30.8	9	5.6	10	0	7
Latino/a	12.5	2	15.4	6	16.7	25	9.1	4
Middle Eastern **	0	0	0	0	11.1	N/A	0	0
Native American	0	1	0	0	0	1	0	0
Multiracial/other	0	0	0	0	0	1	9.1	1
% Gender								
Male	12.5	N/A	69.2	N/A	55.6	N/A	63.6	N/A
Female	87.5	N/A	30.8	N/A	44.4	N/A	36.4	N/A

*Figures for focal students were compiled by us; figures for schools were taken from the state report card. Some categories may not total !00% due to rounding.

**Because Middle Easterners were counted as White at Global Horizons and they are not reported as a separate group in the state report card, we had no way of knowing the actual proportion of Middle Easterners in the larger school population. Participant observations suggested that those of Middle Eastern origin were overrepresented among the focal students at Global Horizons.

Nor could we exactly match the characteristics of focal students with those of their broader school populations. This would perhaps be expected, because the focal students, by study design, were in the top 20 percent of the class. Prior studies make clear the strong relationship between track placement and student socioeconomic status (SES) and race, so we might expect that more highly capitalized students in SES terms would consistently be in higher tracks.[19] This may be the case in general at the schools we studied, but it was not consistently true for the focal students. (See the appendix for additional information about the representativeness and generalizability of the samples.)

Using FRL rates as a proxy for poverty (a common metric in social science research), we found the following: At Chavez in Denver, 85 percent of focal students received FRL as compared to 74 percent of the overall school. The comparable percentages at Southside in Denver were 100 percent (focal students) versus 93 percent (school). Thus, lower-income students were somewhat overrepresented among focal students at these two schools. This means the focal students, who were drawn from the top 20 percent of their respective high school classes at Chavez and Southside, were somewhat more likely than their school populations to be from low-income families. The opposite was the case at Pella and Capital, where the focal students were more likely than their school populations to be from somewhat higher-income (i.e., not qualified for FRL) families. This was especially the case at Capital.

In Denver, the predominant minoritized population was Latino/a, with relatively few students of other minoritized populations represented. A smaller population of Latino/a students (compared to their percentage in the schools) were among our focal students in Denver; in some cases, the differences were large. For example, 25 percent of focal students at Pella were Latino/a versus 65 percent in the broader school population.

In Buffalo, differences were less stark, but the overall pattern remained. At Broadway Science, low-income students, as measured by FRL, were overrepresented among focal students (100 percent versus 77 percent). At STEM Academy, they were underrepresented (54 percent versus 80 percent). At Lincoln, they were also underrepresented but not by very much (73 percent versus 77 percent). At Global Horizons, low-income students, as measured by FRL, were overrepresented among focal students (100 percent versus 86 percent).

In Buffalo, the predominant minoritized population was African American/Black, followed by Latino/a. Focal students in all four Buffalo schools were less likely to be Black than the broader school population. Latino/a students were overrepresented in the focal student category at three of the four schools—the exception being STEM Academy.[20]

Although it would have been ideal to have the focal students better matched to their school populations and the schools better matched to one another, this was not possible, as we were dependent on schools, students, and parents who agreed to participate in the study. We also consciously over-sampled for racial/ethnic diversity *among* those students in the top 20 percent who agreed to participate in the study. What we can say is that in both cities, the focal students tended to be less Black (in Buffalo) and Latino/a (in Denver) than the broader populations of the schools. Put another way, by these measures, the focal students tended to be more diverse than the schools they attended. (See the appendix for a discussion of the demographic characteristics of the school *districts* in our studies compared to other large-city school districts in the United States. In general, our student populations were economically poorer, as measured by FRL rates, and more minoritized, especially Black and Latino/a, than in average large-city districts.)

CHAPTERS IN THIS BOOK

In this book, we discuss what we learned about STEM education reform efforts, students' experiences of high school STEM, and STEM outcomes over the course of almost ten years of research, including in these schools and collecting post-high school follow-up data with focal students. We begin with what we learned during three years (2010–2013)—on the ground, ethnographically—in the eight schools, with specific focus on the ninety-six focal students whom we systematically followed from sophomore to senior year of high school. To these ethnographic data, we added data from follow-up surveys and interviews that we conducted with as many focal students as we could find in 2015 and 2017 through 2019.

Each of the following chapters takes up a key topic in STEM education reform as we learned about it in the Denver and Buffalo schools we studied. As we move through the chapters, we theorize and integrate findings in a comprehensive depiction of the many challenges and some successes of STEM education reform efforts intended for non-privileged, largely minoritized schools and students in the United States. We focus specifically on the mechanisms that produced the outcomes we found.

Chapter 2, "Launching STEM Education Reform in Denver and Buffalo," introduces the efforts to improve STEM education in Denver and

Buffalo just before and during the period of our ethnographic study (2010–2013). By fall 2010, when our study began, the Denver and Buffalo school districts had proposed and begun to implement plans for a few STEM-focused high schools and for STEM enhancements at traditional comprehensive high schools. At that time, we found evidence of increased curricular opportunities for STEM in all four high schools in Denver, although their sustainability in some schools was already in doubt. In Buffalo, we found ambitious plans for more STEM opportunities but few signs of positive change and some evidence that opportunities there were actually declining.

Chapter 3, "Erosion of STEM Opportunities, Especially in Buffalo," takes a closer look at Buffalo and what happened to the ambitious plans for improved STEM opportunities there. In Buffalo, we see clearly the *erosion* of envisioned STEM opportunity structures and the consequences for students. New opportunities were more seriously undermined than in Denver, including being diluted by a form of "shadow capital" that promised but did not deliver higher-level math or science opportunities.

Chapter 4, "Diverting and Outsourcing College and STEM Counseling," reveals how high school guidance counselors' work in the schools in both cities was diverted away from college and career counseling and, in some cases, outsourced to external partnerships and online programs. Attention to students who were most at risk of not graduating became the counselors' highest priority. Addressing their needs left counselors with little time to provide guidance for high-achieving students or for students specifically interested in STEM. In Denver, the schools tried to compensate by outsourcing college counseling to external providers, but as a whole, the reassignment of college counselors to at-risk students diminished opportunities for high-achieving students to explore college options and STEM careers in the schools in both cities.

In chapter 5, "Figured Worlds of Success in High School Math and Science," we turn from *opportunity structures* to *interpretive discourses* ("figured worlds") that circulated among the high-achieving students in our study. We focus on the meanings associated with being successful in math or science in the eight schools. We found "hollowed-out" figured worlds of school math and science that reduced the meaning of success in these subject areas to compliant behavior, high grades, and passing courses. As in the case of shadow capital (chapter 3), hollowed-out figured worlds of STEM were not as potent or enervating in Denver as they were in Buffalo.

Chapter 6, "Educational and Occupational Outcomes," examines the academic and career outcomes of the focal students in our Denver and Buffalo studies. Using data from the three-year high school ethnographic study, six years of post-high school surveys, and follow-up interviews, we charted the high school to postsecondary college and employment trajectories of a subset of the focal students over nine years (2010–2019). These trajectories revealed both expected and unexpected results. As expected given our findings that mechanisms of erosion, diversion, and hollowed-out figured worlds were less stark in Denver than in Buffalo, we found that the Denver focal students for whom we have follow-up data took more advanced math and science courses, attended higher-level colleges, and were more likely to be employed in STEM fields than the focal students in Buffalo. Unexpectedly, given the shared mechanisms of erosion, diversion, and hollowed-out figured worlds across the cities, half of the Denver focal students achieved impressive college and career outcomes.

In chapter 7, "A Closer Look at STEM Trajectories in Denver," we report on the twenty-five focal students in Denver (52 percent of our original Denver sample) who pursued a STEM field in college. Given that these students were not privileged—they represented marginalized groups, low-to-modest-income families, and urban non-criterion public schools—the percentage pursuing some form of STEM in college was impressive and far exceeds conventional expectations.[21] We identify some common patterns in their high school to college trajectories and contrast their trajectories with other focal students in our Denver sample. Of special interest is how the system created by diminished opportunities, diverted counselors, and hollowed-out figured worlds led to such impressive STEM outcomes among the Denver focal students.

In chapter 8, "Minding the Gaps," we focus on the processes by which Denver and Buffalo focal students, two groups generally comparable in demographic characteristics, school characteristics, academic achievement, and interest in STEM when our study began in 2010, had diverged quite dramatically in their college and STEM outcomes by 2019. As the focal students moved through high school and into and beyond college, their experiences of school and STEM accumulated in ways that advantaged the Denver students and disadvantaged the Buffalo students. This pattern of accumulating (dis)advantage had stark implications for these individuals and for the prospects of broadening participation in STEM. We conclude this chapter with some "lessons learned" and ideas for moving forward with STEM education reform.

The final section of the book is an appendix that includes details of the research methodology used in our study.

Launching STEM Education Reform in Denver and Buffalo

"This school is an effort by the community to provide a new facility for our student population to prepare them for the twenty-first century. And, to make sure that they gain access to the resources that other schools may have or that other districts may have had that we hadn't had for many, many years."

These words, from our first interview with the principal of Pella High School, suggest the excitement and optimism with which the STEM-focused schools in Denver launched in 2009–10.[1] New, expanded, and enhanced opportunities for high-level math and science courses were promised, better preparation for college was projected, and greater interest in high-level STEM careers was anticipated. To prepare for these changes, teachers participated in special training sessions in math and science. As the principal of Chavez High School noted in an interview with us: "We have two [new] STEM programs for teachers, which the teachers then bring into the classrooms to support students in classroom instruction. [In partnership with two local colleges, we] applied for opportunities for all those teachers to have [special training] in STEM teaching in the classroom."

As these new programs began, teachers appeared well qualified for their assignments. All the teachers in STEM fields at the two Denver STEM-focused high schools had advanced degrees (at least a master's degree) and were certified (licensed) to teach in their subject areas. All the teachers we interviewed spoke positively about the new programs, about updating and revising their curriculum materials, about planning in teams, and about integrating lessons across disciplines. Yet, despite enthusiasm for STEM reform in these districts and good intentions and hard work on the part of school personnel, the schools faced challenges to the reforms they envisioned.

INCREASING STEM OPPORTUNITIES IN DENVER

A key focus of our study was the school's STEM "opportunity structure"— that is, its provision of resources and people to provide STEM courses and other support for STEM interests and development. In Denver, one highly visible addition to the opportunity structure at the STEM-focused schools was STEM-related courses that had not been offered in predecessor schools. One school added Marine Biology/Oceanography, Environmental Science, and Anatomy/Physiology. Another added Engineering Principles, Engineering Design, Environmental Systems, Anatomy/Physiology, and Urban Horticulture Studies. Both also added AP courses in math and science and an International Baccalaureate (IB) program (an internationally recognized program of high-level classes and requirements, including in math and science, leading to an IB diploma). These additions were reflective of notable expansion in the schools' opportunity structures with respect to STEM.

The Denver schools also joined with a range of partners to add enrichment to their math and science curricula. Partners included Johns Hopkins Talent Development (a model for gifted education); Teach for Success (a model for improved instruction); nearby colleges that provided math and science afterschool programming, guest speakers, and college visits; local engineering businesses (offering internships and workplace visits); the MESA (Mathematics, Engineering, Science Achievement) program for special classes devoted to STEM projects; and the ALEKS (Assessment and Learning in Knowledge Spaces) online program for individualized math learning and assessment. Teachers also established afterschool math clubs and a club for Hispanic engineering students.

The Denver schools also implemented double class periods for math ("doubling up") so that students could take two math classes every day. This system allowed students to take both Algebra II and Geometry in tenth grade and, if successful, take Precalculus and Calculus in eleventh grade and twelfth grade, respectively.

These opportunities were especially noteworthy at the two STEM-focused schools because their predecessor schools had not offered anything of the kind. They generated excitement and contributed to increased enrollment at the two schools, but when compared to the two traditional high schools in Denver, there was surprisingly little difference. Upon initiation of the new STEM-focused schools, the traditional high schools also responded to calls for STEM education reform and took steps to enhance STEM opportunities for their students.

OPPORTUNITIES IN STEM-FOCUSED VERSUS COMPREHENSIVE HIGH SCHOOLS IN DENVER AND BUFFALO

In light of the attempt of STEM-focused schools to broaden opportunities for STEM, we expected to find differences in STEM opportunities when we compared STEM-focused and comprehensive high schools. Certainly, the STEM-focused schools created the *impression* that they would offer more STEM than the comprehensive schools. But several indicators tell a different story. Table 2.1 shows high school graduation requirements for the four Denver schools.

TABLE 2.1 *High school graduation requirements (required credits*) by school, Denver*

	CHAVEZ (STEM)	PELLA (STEM)	SOUTHSIDE (COMPREHENSIVE)	CAPITAL (COMPREHENSIVE)
Language Arts	4	4	4	4
Mathematics	3	3	4	4
Science	3	3	4	4
Social Studies	3	3	3	3
Physical Education	1	1	1	1
Health	0.5	0	0	0
Arts/Tech/CTE	2.5	0.5	1	1
Electives	5	8.5	8	8
Total Required	22	23	25	25

*One credit is equivalent to one academic year of coursework.

Interestingly, the comprehensive schools required *more* math and science for graduation than the new STEM-focused schools. Where the two STEM-focused schools required three math course credits and three science course credits for high school graduation, the comprehensive schools required four in both math and science. Further, the higher requirements at the two comprehensive high schools in Denver aligned more closely with four-year college requirements, which in Colorado call for four years of high school mathematics.

Curious whether the same pattern appeared in Buffalo, we examined the graduation requirements there. Table 2.2 shows that in Buffalo, there were no differences in the number of math and science course credits required for graduation at the four schools.

The tables make clear that despite the intended focus on STEM in the STEM-focused schools, there were relatively few differences in science or math requirements for graduation across the eight schools in our study. In Denver, the STEM requirements (math and science) were higher in the comprehensive schools than in the STEM-focused schools. In Buffalo, they were the same in both school types.

Course offerings "on the books" provided another indicator of differences between STEM-focused and comprehensive schools in our study.

TABLE 2.2 *High school graduation requirements* (required credits) by school, Buffalo*

	BROADWAY SCIENCE ACADEMY (STEM)	STEM ACADEMY (STEM)	GLOBAL HORIZONS (COMPREHENSIVE)	LINCOLN (COMPREHENSIVE)
Language Arts	4	4	4	4
Mathematics	3	3	3	3
Science	3	3	3	3
Social Studies	4	4	4	4
Physical Education	2	2	2	2
Health	0.5	0.5	0.5	0.5
Arts/Tech/CTE	1	1	1	1
Electives	4.5	4.5	4.5	4.5
Total Required	22	22	22	22

*New York State also requires students to pass Regents Comprehensive Examinations in the following areas: math (1), science (1), social studies (2), and English (1).

During the six years (2006–2012) immediately preceding and including our study period, the total number of math and science courses officially offered at three of the Denver schools increased, as did the number of advanced courses, including honors (considered more advanced than regular courses but not as rigorous as AP or IB); see table 2.3.

The increases were greater than can be explained by enrollment increases alone.[2] At Chavez (STEM), math course offerings increased by 36 percent and science offerings by 25 percent while enrollment went up by only 17 percent. At Southside (comprehensive), where enrollment increased by 10 percent, and Capital (comprehensive), where enrollment increased by 16 percent, the number of math courses remained almost the same, but the number of advanced math courses more than doubled at both schools. In science at Southside, the number of science courses increased by 30 percent, and the number of advanced science courses by 500 percent. At Capital, the number of science courses increased by 100 percent and the number of advanced science courses more than tripled. Thus, it appears that students were being offered more STEM course opportunities and more advanced opportunities than previously.

TABLE 2.3 *Math and science course offerings over time, Denver*

	MATH	MATH	SCIENCE	SCIENCE	TOTAL ENROLL	TOTAL ENROLL
	2006–07	2012–13	2006–07	2012–13	2006–07	2012
Chavez (STEM)	11	15	12	15	1,492	1,748
	2 AP	4 H	3 H	2 H		
		5 IB	1 AP	5 IB		
Pella (STEM)	NA	6	NA	11	2,512	2,398
		2 IB		2 H		
				3 IB		
Southside (comprehensive)	10	10	10	13	1,605	1,764
	1 AP	4 H	1 AP	4 H		
		1 AP		2 AP		
Capital (comprehensive)	15	16	10	20	2,258	2,383
	3 AP	3 H	3 AP	5 H		
		4 AP		5 AP		

Source: Data come from course catalogs and scheduling materials from each school.

Note: Cells with numbers only = total number of courses offered; NA = not available; AP = Advanced Placement; IB = International Baccalaureate (including Middle Years program/pre-IB classes); H = Honors.

But again, these increases occurred at both STEM-focused and comprehensive high schools.

Data on course offerings in the Buffalo schools could not be directly compared to Denver.[3] But it is clear that the increases seen in Denver did not occur in Buffalo, and as was the case in Denver, there were few differences between STEM-focused and comprehensive schools. Much smaller in size than the Denver schools, the Buffalo schools offered fewer higher-level math and science courses in the form of AP and Regents courses.[4] These course offerings remained fairly stable over the course of our study at both the STEM-focused and comprehensive schools in Buffalo; they did not show the notable increases seen in Denver. Table 2.4 shows the course offerings in Buffalo during the period of our study and indicates whether math and science courses were non-Regents (NR), Regents (R), or Advanced Placement (AP).

In 2010, Broadway Science offered six Regents courses in math and science—Biology, Earth Science, Algebra I, Geometry, Algebra II/ Trigonometry, and Precalculus—but offered no AP courses. In 2012, Broadway Science continued to offer the same Regents courses and added Regents Chemistry. However, non-Regents courses in environmental science and biopharmacy were no longer offered, and there

TABLE 2.4 *Math and science course offerings over time, Buffalo*

	MATH	MATH	SCIENCE	SCIENCE	TOTAL ENROLL	TOTAL ENROLL
	2010–11	2012–13	2010–11	2012–13	2010–11	2012–13
Broadway Science Academy (STEM)	1 NR 4 R	1 NR 4 R	5 NR* 2 R	3 NR** 3 R	610	388
STEM Academy (STEM)	4 R	5 R	1 NR 3 R 2 AP	4 NR 3 R 2 AP	249	274
Global Horizons (comprehensive)	3R	1 NR 2 R	3 R 1 AP	2 NR 2 R	288	243
Lincoln (comprehensive)	4R	4R	1 NR 3 R	1 NR 3 R	848	661

Source: Data from course catalogs and scheduling materials from each school.

Note: NR = non-Regents (there is no state exam at the conclusion of the course, and it is therefore less rigorous than a Regents-level course); R = Regents; AP = Advanced Placement.

*Non-Regents science courses at Broadway included HOT, Forensics, and Biopharmacy in 2010–11.
**Non-Regents science courses at Broadway included HOT and Forensics in 2012–13.

were, as in previous years, no AP courses. Global Horizons, a compre-hensive school, also offered six Regents courses in 2010: Biology, Chem-istry, Earth Science, Algebra, Algebra II/Trigonometry, and Geometry. It also offered one AP course, Biology. By 2012, there were no AP science or math courses offered at Global Horizons, and the number of Regents courses had dropped to four (Biology, Earth Science, Algebra I, and Ge-ometry). Lincoln, the other comprehensive school in Buffalo, similarly had no AP courses on offer in 2010 or 2012, and its math and science Regents offerings remained the same over the three-year period (seven Regents courses were offered: Biology, Chemistry, Earth Science, Alge-bra I, Geometry, Algebra II/Trigonometry, and Precalculus). While the Buffalo schools did offer enough Regents courses to ensure their stu-dents were eligible for a Regents diploma (as required for graduation by New York State education law), there were some instances where, after eleventh grade, students were left with no higher-level math or science options if they already had enough credits to graduate.

Another striking feature shown in table 2.4 is that only STEM Acad-emy consistently offered AP STEM courses from 2010 to 2012 (in biol-ogy and environmental science). And it expanded its Regents courses in math by one over this period.

By these measures, the study schools in Denver were more suc-cessful than those in Buffalo at increasing available course offerings in math and science, and particularly higher-level course offerings in these subjects. However, these data must be interpreted cautiously.[5] We were not able to accurately compare the content or quality of the various offerings; thus, we cannot assume that an honors or AP course in Col-orado is necessarily more advanced than, say, a Regents course in New York, nor can we assume that the content or quality of a given course is consistent across school sites. We can say that during the period of our study in these schools, math and science course options increased somewhat in both STEM-focused and comprehensive schools in Den-ver and not in Buffalo; and in neither city did STEM-focused schools exhibit any decidedly greater focus on math and science courses than comprehensive high schools that served roughly comparable student populations.

Thus, our initial expectation that the STEM-focused schools would offer notably more STEM opportunities than the comprehensive schools was not borne out. Much more significant were the differences between the schools in the two cities. We examine these differences further in subsequent chapters.

In the next section of this chapter, we take a closer look at Chavez High School, one of the two STEM-focused schools in Denver. This case reveals in some detail how STEM reform efforts fell short of expectations in a STEM-focused school.

OPPORTUNITIES AT STEM-FOCUSED CHAVEZ HIGH SCHOOL IN DENVER

Chavez High was reorganized as an academy school shortly before our study began. The reorganization was part of the district's efforts to improve education overall and STEM education in particular. At Chavez, the Science and Technology Academy was formed. The primary purpose of the academy structure was to group students by career interest—in this case, science or engineering—and deliver to the group both general education courses, such as math, science, and English, and specialized courses in the career interest area. Teachers assigned to an academy had responsibility for integrating a specialty area focus into the general education courses as well as teaching the specialty courses.

As we began to spend time at Chavez, it soon became clear that implementing the academy structure would be difficult. Teachers and students had a general understanding of the academies' purpose (to group students into classes by career interest area), but they struggled to make sense of its organization. One student explained the purpose:

> Pretty much, the academies are broken down to what you want to do in life, so, like, where you want to go in your careers. So, you have the Visual and Performing Arts; that's like if you wanna be an artist, an actor, a musician, and all that stuff. There is Science and Tech, and that is for being a doctor . . . There is Global

Business, which is what I'm in, and it's coursework of getting you into business.

But many expressed confusion about how the academy structure actually worked. Jésus, who intended to choose the Early College Academy (ostensibly for students wishing to earn community college credit while simultaneously completing high school), did not end up there. (All participant names in both cities are pseudonyms.) Jésus explained:

Last year I was in Early College and then this year I started off as IB [International Baccalaureate]. I didn't even switch or anything, they didn't even tell me. They just gave me my schedule and all my classes were IB.

Nora did not understand what it meant to be in an academy:

I'm in Early College right now, [but] I have a class in every single academy . . . I have Algebra in Arts Academy, I have English in Early College, I have Chemistry in IB, and then I have Civics in Science and Tech.

Nancy, who wanted to switch into Early College, ended up staying in Visual and Performing Arts because the staff lost her paperwork: "I was supposed to move this year to Early College, but they messed up, and they couldn't find my paperwork, so I stayed in Arts."

There was also widespread misunderstanding among students about the meaning of "Early College."[6] Although its name refers to an academy for relatively strong high school students who want to be better prepared for four-year colleges by earning community college credit while still in high school, at Chavez it was more of a remedial academy to prepare struggling students for community college attendance. Many students, including Nancy, understood it as a special academy for those who wanted to attend four-year colleges, as she did. In Nancy's case, her college plans would have been disadvantaged by a switch to the more remedial Early College program at Chavez, although she did not realize it.

Such seemingly random assignment to academies characterized the school lives of teachers as well. One teacher said:

> It's supposed to be an academy school. So, I'm supposed to have only students from Science and Tech, and those Science and Tech students are supposed to go from class to class together. All in one wing. That's not how it's happened, because . . . the class sizes are so big that they're . . . putting kids wherever. I have a class that's all kids from another academy.

A science teacher described being inexplicably assigned to the Visual and Performing Arts Academy:

> Honestly, our kids, every kid that comes into this school has to go through the same classes . . . and not every kid is meant to go through the same classes. So, I think that is something that needs to be remedied. The goal is if you are in the Arts Academy, you are more aimed at taking theater classes, or you are a writer, or you want to go on to more in those areas. . . . I am in the Arts Academy right now, by default, not for any specific reason. I'm hoping to get into Science and Tech next year.

Another teacher, in math, said this about the classes she and her math colleagues taught:

> So, my colleagues and I, I am in the Science and Tech Academy. Ms. [ ] is in Early College and Ms. [ ] is in Arts, but we teach the exact same thing, pretty much the exact same way. It's an academy by name only.

Clearly, implementing the academy structure at Chavez was a struggle, and considerable confusion about its purpose and value ensued.

While there were multiple reasons for these problems, several were especially salient. For one thing, the academy structure was predicated on the idea that roughly equal numbers of students would choose each academy. This was not the case: for example, many more students chose Early College (often because they misunderstood its intent at Chavez) than the other academies. Thus, some academies were over-enrolled and others under-enrolled. Teachers were reassigned to classes based on enrollment rather than academy focus.

Second, as one teacher pointed out, the school was simultaneously trying to implement the new academy structure and align the curriculum with new state-imposed core standards. She explained:

> So, there are new core standards. We need to kind of incorporate those, but they kind of mixed up the [academy] curriculum in order to do that, and I think that the teachers, they aren't listened to [regarding the problems] . . . and so I think there's a lot of people [going in a lot of different directions].

In fact, *the requirements for graduation and core standards were at odds with the academy goals.* While the academy structure called for broader opportunities and more flexibility for students to concentrate on individual interests, including STEM, graduation requirements insisted on a specific number of courses in specific subjects, while core standards demanded that teachers concentrate on specific math, reading, and science content on which students would be proficiency-tested by the state. A school's failure to offer all students the necessary courses for graduation, or to offer struggling students remedial courses to raise test scores, could result in serious sanctions, such as limited or no salary increases for teachers. Sanctioned schools could also be reorganized or closed and teachers reassigned or laid off. Thus, failure to offer courses for graduation or to raise test scores in proficiency areas covered by the core standards was much more consequential for teachers and the school than were the academy goals. In the case of the academies, no one in authority outside the school measured or even paid much attention to whether the academy goals were implemented or achieved. Even the principal at Chavez seemed to dismiss the importance of the academy structure. He said:

> We think science and math are the cornerstones, if you are talking about kids . . . math is the keystone to anything you want to do academically . . . [but] we are working on writing this year, 'cause we believe that is our quickest 'bang for our buck' [i.e., most likely to produce improvement in test scores]—a kid has got to learn how to read and write, but once that is done, then we are shifting our focus to math . . . getting our math program in order.

While more than the expected number of students enrolled in the Early College Academy, fewer than hoped for chose the Science and Technology Academy or the Liberal Arts Academy in which the IB (advanced) program was housed. Thus, the school actually taught only one honors course in science (Chemistry) for eleventh-grade students and no honors courses for students in twelfth grade. The school did not teach any honors or AP math or science courses for eleventh or twelfth graders; there was one IB math and one IB science course offered to eleventh- and twelfth-grade students in the IB program, but the courses did not count toward an IB diploma, because the IB program as a whole was too small to justify hiring teachers for all the courses necessary for the IB diploma. In 2013–14, Chavez canceled the IB program completely, although the advanced math and science courses remained.

Another problem at Chavez was extremely high staff turnover. Both teachers and students were left uncertain about who would be teaching what and how to plan. One teacher explained:

> We have a high turnover of staff on a regular basis and in the administration. This year, all of the administration is new except for one assistant principal. [When I arrived in 2011] teachers were very skeptical about administration, along with students. And students had the feeling that it doesn't really matter what we do because it will be somebody new in another year.

Similar processes occurred at Pella (the other STEM-focused school in Denver). There, an orientation toward STEM was supposed to permeate the core courses in the Engineering and Health/Medicine Academies and support electives offered in each academy. However, before the end of the first year of academies (also the first year of our study), teachers and administrators at Pella struggled to implement the new organization. As happened at Chavez, students and parents were confused by academy labels and the inconsistent availability of both academy-oriented core courses and academy electives. School administrators and teachers struggled to reconcile the academy agenda with other reforms mandated by the district or state, specifically standards-based learning and graduation requirements. Finally, administrative issues of class size, teacher qualifications, student scheduling, pressure to improve graduation rates and test scores, and complaints from parents, students, and teachers undid efforts to group and teach students by academy.

Both schools had abandoned their academies by 2012 but had plans to reinvent them and bring them back in 2013–14. At Chavez, the principal told us: "Next year, we are shifting, we are going to a [new] academy format. We are going to . . . smaller academies." The new idea was to have all incoming ninth graders placed in a Freshman Academy with a set of core (math, science, English language arts, and social studies) teachers. At the end of ninth grade, students would then elect to join an engineering academy, a health science academy, or a liberal arts academy. According to the principal, the goals of these new academies would include a renewed focus on math, science, and college preparation.

New academies were also planned at Pella for the 2013–14 school year. According to yet another new principal there:

> We are going to sort of reinvent the academy. But it's not going to be something you are automatically placed in [or choose to be in], but you earn your way into it by meeting a certain threshold. We'll let them [the teachers] figure out what the thresholds are, so then it [the academy] is sort of like a club—a cool club that's academically motivated, it's a badge of honor: "I'm in the STEM academy, cool!"

Despite these plans, Chavez did not reinstate an academy structure. Pella implemented a new academy structure but dropped the plan to include a STEM-related academy.

GOOD INTENTIONS ARE NOT ENOUGH

In the United States today, inclusive STEM-focused schools are an appealing educational reform. These schools are increasingly promoted as a means of improving educational experiences and occupational outcomes for low-income and minoritized students, and the number of STEM-focused schools is growing rapidly.[7] In our study, we found enthusiasm for STEM-focused schools among students and parents, as well as good ideas and good intentions among district- and school-level administrators, teachers, and counselors. All the schools we studied were trying to get better, including trying to improve the opportunity structure for STEM.

But the STEM-focused schools we studied did not deliver on their promises. They promised STEM courses and programs of study not offered at their predecessor schools or at other public schools in their districts. They promised more rigorous and more advanced STEM courses. They promised extra efforts, particularly in math, to encourage students to pursue a coherent math sequence, culminating in Calculus in grade 12. New STEM courses and programs were added at both schools, but they were hard to implement in conjunction with uneven enrollments, state core standards, and accountability pressures to increase achievement scores and graduation rates. Chavez, the STEM-focused school we focus on in this chapter, was also plagued by high staff turnover and a low reservoir of community support. Within three years, the academy structure at Chavez collapsed, leaving only one IB course in math and one in science per year for eleventh and twelfth graders. Some of these conditions also existed at Pella, the other STEM-focused school in Denver. Conflicts arose between academy goals, state standards, and achievement and graduation goals. Although staff turnover was lower and community support somewhat higher at Pella than at Chavez, Pella's academy structure also collapsed within three years and the proposed replacement academy structure did not include any STEM-related academies. And, as comparisons with the two STEM schools in Buffalo reveal (see tables 2.3 and 2.4), the STEM-focused schools there also were not able to deliver on their promises (more about this in chapter 3).

In contrast to what we found in our STEM-focused schools, Sharon Lynch and colleagues identified fourteen components that contribute to *successful* inclusive STEM high schools.[8] The components were based on literature promoting inclusive STEM high schools (ISHSs) as well as evidence from "exemplar" ISHSs—schools that were "especially successful in producing positive [STEM] outcomes for their diverse student populations."[9] These schools look very different from the ones we found in Denver and Buffalo. In the schools we studied, key components such as rigorous and integrated courses in all four STEM disciplines, innovative technology, and autonomy from school district requirements were not feasible and only barely conceivable.

The STEM-focused schools we studied tried to add more courses and more advanced courses in STEM; they tried to integrate STEM into non-STEM courses; they tried to improve STEM instruction and teacher training; and they tried to establish university partnerships and concurrent college enrollment programs to enhance STEM offerings. But, for the most part, their efforts could not be sustained.

Notably, none of our STEM schools could focus on getting better at STEM alone. They all faced multiple issues at once: large numbers of "low performing" students as determined by standardized tests, disappointing graduation rates, students with limited English proficiency, competing reform agendas, a limited "college-going culture," and teachers and other staff stretched thin. These issues—and the way the schools did or could address them—set limits on what STEM opportunities could be provided and sustained over time. Graduation requirements were set by the state, and in all our schools, the number and distribution of courses to meet these requirements were mandated. Further, high school graduation rates were used as a school accountability measure, and one that these schools could not take for granted given the "low performing" standardized scores of the students they served. The schools had to offer math and science courses that low performing students could handle and pass; they had to offer courses they believed would raise achievement test scores. Only then could they consider advanced or specialized STEM courses. When advanced courses were offered, they had to enroll sufficient numbers of students to justify a teacher, and if numbers of qualified students did not exist or declined, then the advanced courses had to be canceled. Both the STEM-focused and the comprehensive schools in our study tried to include more math and science—in some cases, by doubling up on math courses or offering more sections of honors or AP math and science; in others, by insisting that students take "hard" math and science courses even if they did not want to.[10] But if, in the end, the courses did not enroll a requisite number of students, they could not be sustained. At some schools, concurrent enrollment at nearby community colleges was an alternative for students who wanted to take more or advanced STEM courses, but given the remedial nature of many community college courses, this is not necessarily a marked improvement. Further, in most cases students had to provide their own transportation to community college, and many in this population were unable to do so.

In both cities, the attempt to improve STEM opportunity structures for low-income and minoritized students by reorganizing struggling urban schools to focus on STEM floundered after very little time. In Buffalo, STEM opportunities constricted at all four sample schools within a three-year period. In Denver, the academies collapsed during the same three-year period, taking their STEM strands with them. In Denver, the comprehensive high schools seemed to be doing somewhat better, although analysis of a larger sample including student outcomes is necessary to support this claim (see chapter 6).

CHAPTER 3

Erosion of STEM Opportunities, Especially in Buffalo

"Even next year, most likely, they're [the STEM classes] gonna go away. Most likely Anatomy will be gone, AP Environmental will probably be gone, and Pre-calculus will probably be gone, because I don't think we'll have fifteen bodies to put in those seats."[1] (STEM Academy guidance counselor)

In Buffalo, we see even more clearly the notable *erosion* of enhanced opportunity structures that were envisioned and put in place when the STEM-focused schools first opened.[2] By erosion, we mean the diminution of opportunities over the period of time that marked our three-year ethnographic investigation. Although primarily a scientific term (e.g., erosion by wind gradually carves grooves in rocks), erosion in this context refers to the chipping away of both the initial vision for STEM and the enhanced opportunities that were put in place when Buffalo embraced STEM school reform. This erosion fundamentally altered and compromised initially envisioned changes.

OPPORTUNITIES FOR STEM REFORM IN BUFFALO

When our study began, public support for the Buffalo schools was somewhat less effusive than in Denver, but district efforts were underway to improve the schools via STEM education. An op-ed piece in the local newspaper noted the creation of STEM programs in Buffalo and declared, "The school system can be a magnet to draw people back to the city and reverse urban decline."[3] While there was some community skepticism about the district's ability to successfully implement STEM reforms, the news outlets commended the creation of these new programs and parents and students expressed strong interest in pursuing them.

The data we report in this chapter come primarily from our work at the two STEM-focused schools in Buffalo: STEM Academy and Broadway Science. Both were designated "STEM-focused schools" by the school district. At STEM Academy, students were supposed to take Algebra and Biology (typically ninth-grade courses) as well as US History (typically an eleventh-grade course) in grade 8. The idea was to accelerate students so that they could take AP math and science classes beginning in tenth and eleventh grades. Originally, all students were expected to take at least two AP classes in addition to Regents courses and examinations required by New York State for high school graduation.

Also, certain teachers at STEM Academy used their personal connections with faculty at local universities to develop partnerships to improve math or science education. One central administrator stated that a goal was to make the school truly "science and math focused," and continued:

> I have seven teachers there [at STEM Academy]. When I look at Melissa [science teacher] . . . Melissa is very strong . . . and she takes kids out to [the university], and they work in labs out there. Susan . . . she does a lot with kids out there too, and she has grad students coming into her class [as volunteers]. . . . The teachers in the Science Department . . . truly have a vision of what we are looking to change, but now it is going to be getting everybody in the building onto that vision.

The second school, Broadway Science, opened in the 2005–2006 academic year. The new school recruited students by contacting parents of middle school students with high grades in math and science and offering them the opportunity to attend the school and participate in a specialized science program, the Biopharmacy program. The program was intended to prepare students for higher education leading to high-level STEM-related jobs, particularly in research. The school also offered a "nursing" program—officially known as the HOT program

(Health Occupations Technology); this program was intended to pre-pare students for higher education leading to a job as a CNA.

In these ways, both STEM Academy and Broadway Science opened with great enthusiasm for planned enhancement of STEM opportuni-ties. There were strong feelings that STEM-focused programs, includ-ing partnerships with local universities and colleges at both schools, could be a pipeline to four-year colleges and high-level STEM careers for low-income and minoritized students.

In both cities, the teachers at the STEM-focused schools appeared to be well qualified to take on these new tasks. All the math, science, and engineering teachers had advanced degrees (at least a master's de-gree) and were certified (licensed) to teach in their subject areas. All the teachers we interviewed talked enthusiastically about updating and re-vising curriculum materials, planning in teams, and integrating lessons across disciplines as part of the upgrades to STEM education at their schools. As in Denver, we also included in our sample two traditional comprehensive schools that similarly planned to enhance offerings in STEM; we refer to one of these schools, Global Horizons, in this chapter.

EROSION OF OPPORTUNITIES IN BUFFALO

In this chapter, we look closely at the reform efforts in the Buffalo schools, with an eye toward illuminating the mechanisms through which initial vision and early efforts to enhance STEM opportunities were eroded during the period of our ethnographic study (2010–2013). This *on-the-ground* erosion resulted in substantially altered opportu-nity structures that markedly departed from both the vision and initial enactment of intended reforms. Here, we identify three mechanisms through which curricular erosion took place: erosion of high-level course offerings in math and science, programmatic erosion, and ero-sion of within-course content.

Erosion of High-Level Course Offerings in Math and Science

STEM Academy opened in 2006. Its objective (as per its website) was to be a state-of-the-art science and technology school: to offer increased numbers of high-level courses in math, science, and technology; to emphasize extracurricular opportunities in STEM; and to prepare all students to be "college ready," enabling a smooth transition to college.[4] When the principal arrived in 2007, the school was operating from a temporary site (an old, run-down school building with insufficient space), and a notable lack of STEM opportunities prompted an initiative to reconceive and reemphasize the school's intended STEM focus. During summer 2012, STEM Academy transitioned to a newly renovated, technologically enhanced building. Just prior to the move, we interviewed one of the counselors, whose perspective is instructive:

> RESEARCHER: Are there special programs or opportunities available to students to encourage them to go into STEM fields?
>
> SCHOOL COUNSELOR: Really very few as far as our . . . name's sake [given the school's name: STEM Academy]. It is the principal's primary mission this year [to make the school more STEM focused] . . . If you talk with the kids you will hear that we have science and math Olympiad[s]. We had Weather Bug [an online interactive tool for teaching math, science, and geography]. One of the science teachers has worked with a professor at [State University] in the Physics Department. Not a lot on the math. *It has mainly been science focused, which, to be honest, is where we are going to head, because math for a lot of students is difficult* [our emphasis], and so to accelerate kids in math or to offer AP math to students is pretty [iffy] . . . I don't even think honors [classes] would do that; it is pretty much not realistic. I mean, you have your occasional eleventh grader—I can think of two right now—who are math whizzes, but you are talking about two [students] in the whole class. You can't have two [students] in a class, and it is unfortunate because then those two kids in every grade miss out. We don't have a Statistics course for fourth year because there are just no bodies to put in there.

Although the counselor began by suggesting that if we "talk with the kids" we "will hear that we have science and math Olympiad[s]," the fact is that we never once heard a word about either of the Olympi-ads or any other special STEM-related activities in the school. This was in spite of the fact that we asked about these activities in interviews and informal encounters with students on a consistent basis over the three years of our within-school ethnographic study.

The counselor went on to talk about shifting attention away from high-level math courses because so few students were "realistically" prepared to take these courses. As the counselor explained, if there were only two students each year who were prepared to take honors classes (at best), it was not feasible for the school to offer advanced math courses.

To be clear, the school did open with the full intention of offering high-level math courses, including AP Calculus, AP Statistics, and AP Computer Science. The school also promised to offer high-level science offerings, specifically AP Chemistry and AP Physics. Yet, in argu-ing that most of the students did not do well in math and that they were not even at the level of honors, much less AP, higher-level math and any science courses that depended on some math quickly came to be construed by teachers and counselors as "out of reach" of the student body, even for those in the top 20 percent of the class, includ-ing our focal students. The initial vision to offer higher-level math courses was quickly compromised, and the school simply stopped of-fering them.

Nonetheless, as the counselor explained, STEM Academy intended to continue to focus on science, which was, she explained, "where we are going to head, because math for a lot of students is difficult." When the counselor stated that STEM Academy would increasingly prioritize science but not high-level math, her words represented a substantial scaling back and a marked shift in the original vision for the school. This shift in vision, and the accompanying diversion of resources to students who struggled with math at the expense of students who *might* successfully engage in high-level math courses, had import-ant consequences for the high school opportunity structure, as only *nonmathematized* science courses—that is, those that do not assume a certain level of math competence—were made available in what was intended to be a school that would prepare students for STEM majors in four-year colleges and, ultimately, high-level careers in STEM.

Programmatic Erosion

At Broadway Science, quick erosion of the initially enhanced high school opportunity structure was even more evident, exhibiting a distinct pattern of what we call *programmatic erosion*. Such erosion was preceded by the elimination of high-level math courses, particularly Precalculus, which, although available the year the school opened, was offered *in name only* by year two of our study. When Broadway Science opened, a key programmatic aspect was the opportunity for top students to study in its university-linked Biopharmacy program. This was Broadway Science's first STEM program, and it was expected to anchor the newly opened school. As the assistant principal stated: "We envisioned this to be a science-based school with Biopharmacy."

The stated goal of the Biopharmacy program, like the expressed goal of STEM Academy as a whole, was to prepare students, especially those who were low income and minoritized, for STEM coursework in a four-year college, a major in STEM, and a STEM career. Stated Dr. Burdette, founding member of the Biopharmacy program and faculty member at a Research I university, the goal was to deliver "a strong chemistry program with a lot of pharmacy-related topics; computer science [enabling students] to write computer programs and understand the basics of computing; genetics; [and] biology."[5] According to Burdette, when students completed the program they were "prepared to enter STEM in college and later a career—to be involved in some aspect of biopharmaceutical sciences."

For the first few years, teachers and counselors reported that the program operated with some success, and several of its graduates went on to major in science fields at four-year colleges. Students in the early years of the school took a required course in biopharmacy. In 2010, year one of our study, the course was offered. It was a challenging course required of all students in this advanced program and part of a dedicated within-school science track. By year two of our study, the course was no longer offered, having been replaced by additional sections of remedial science electives, such as Forensics, which was part of the CTE program.[6] This shift in program offerings marked another move away from high-level science courses aimed at positioning students for STEM in four-year postsecondary institutions.

This early erosion of math course offerings as evidenced in the second year of our study signaled the soon-to-be end of the promised Bio-pharmacy program. By summer 2011, the program was "suspended," and what was conceptualized and advertised as a high-level opportunity for STEM in college and career was officially closed in 2012. Mr. Koch, the lead science teacher, reflected on the program:

> My first group of twenty-four kids was the best group I ever had. A few of them are in [university] science degree programs now. These kids went to internships. The first . . . years of this program they went places; they had opportunities; they had their own laptops. They were motivated. They understood what the program was about. And, some time along the way, the program just fell apart.

While Mr. Koch said that "the program just fell apart," Mr. Burdette suggested something different. He stated:

> The principal at the time when the program was booming had really good communication with [State University] and was a big believer in the program, and then . . . the next principal that came on . . . his focus entirely was the students who were really struggling because the emphasis of the superintendent [changed] . . . He [the superintendent] was being criticized for the low graduation rates and things like that. So, the next time I went to the school to meet with them . . . the really high-end STEM program was already gone. Yes, Biopharmacy was gone because the principal was putting every bit of emphasis into helping the kids who were failing . . . Our interaction with the school changed from what we envisioned as supporting the STEM program but also helping the rest of the school, to the entire school focusing on improving graduation rates and what could we do to help with that. . . . [The new principal

and superintendent] thought that CTE programs were their path to graduation and to career . . . and the Biopharmacy program was therefore disbanded. I think the retirement of [the original] principal was a major piece, and the new principal's marching orders came directly from the superintendent.

Like the situation in Denver, the Buffalo schools were under increased pressure to produce higher graduation rates, thereby staying off the Persistently Lowest-Achieving (PLA) list—a designation that meant sanctions and possible school closure.[7] Despite any differences with respect to the stated reasons for program closure, the consequences for the original vision of the newly opened STEM school were clear, as the *nature* of the school's commitment to particular kinds of STEM futures for the attending population of low-income and minoritized students fundamentally changed. Students could now pursue STEM programs *only* in the CTE track.

For example, although the Biopharmacy program had been housed in the Science Department, both the subsequently added Forensics and HOT programs were CTE programs, with little connection to academic science or math, as per participant observation in classrooms and discussions with faculty.[8] In addition, whereas the Biopharmacy program sought to connect students with a four-year university and a STEM major, the HOT and Forensic programs were pathways to two-year institutions or entry-level work as, for instance, CNAs (HOT) and security guards (Forensics).

Forensics was also not able to actualize its original vision. Although envisioned as a CTE track *science option* that included scientific forensic work, thereby scaffolding entrance to a scientifically based two-year degree program such as Law Enforcement Associate in Applied Science, this vision quickly deteriorated. Forensics became STEM *in name only*, linked to a two-year program in general law enforcement rather than to forensic science. In fact, the program was physically located several floors away from the science and math faculty and had no formal connection to these departments or teachers at all, a fact that the science and math teachers pointed out to us.

To be clear, we are not against high school programs aimed at job training and entrance to two-year colleges in STEM. However, the elimination of Biopharmacy and the redirection of resources to HOT, along with a particular version of Forensics that funneled students into jobs as security guards rather than as forensic scientists, represent a substantial shift away from the originally stated mission of the school. In the case of Broadway Science, we see the elimination of a program specifically designed to create futures in high-level college and STEM careers with accompanying redirection of emphasis toward low-wage labor positions.

Although we draw our primary examples from Broadway Science and STEM Academy, these mechanisms of erosion, also evident to some degree in the Denver inclusive STEM-focused schools, can be further explored in a close look at Global Horizons, the Buffalo comprehensive school that similarly intended to enhance math and science offerings and career possibilities in STEM. The situation at Global Horizons illustrates not only erosion from higher-level math and science offerings but also diminution of course content *within existing courses*.

Erosion of Within-Course Content

In year two of our study (2011–2012), the existing Algebra II/Trigonometry Regents-level course at Global Horizons was replaced with the less challenging non-Regents Algebra II/Trigonometry course.[9] In addition, participant observation data revealed that teachers further eroded course content by teaching only *half* of the yearlong course during the full year. As a result, students gained *no* exposure to trigonometry in a course that was supposed to cover this material. As one math teacher noted, "They can't handle the trig, so all I covered was algebra." This was confirmed by observational data, which indicated that teachers, and therefore students, spent a lot of time reviewing both Algebra I and Algebra II content rather than attending to trig. As Trigonometry is a prerequisite for Precalculus, and Precalculus and Calculus are prerequisites for many STEM majors in a four-year college, students were effectively closed out of higher-level STEM options.

As argued earlier, the presence of high-level coursework in high school math and science is key to a well-functioning opportunity structure for STEM. However, instead of bolstering possibilities for success in these challenging classes in line with envisioned inclusive STEM-focused schools and programs, the school personnel in Buffalo quickly altered their own envisioned and initially expanded opportunity structure via one or more of the following mechanisms: (1) offering a less demanding version of a particular math or science course by offering it at the non-Regents level rather than the Regents level, or offering a "regular" course rather than the initially envisioned and expanded corpus of AP courses; (2) substantially diminishing course content within a given course by skipping key portions of the curriculum, such as trigonometry in an Algebra II/Trigonometry course; (3) no longer offering critically important four-year college gatekeeping courses, such as Chemistry, Physics, Precalculus, and Calculus; (4) eliminating high-level STEM-linked programs such as Biopharmacy that were intentionally aimed at four-year college entrance and subsequent high-level STEM majors and careers, and replacing them with lower-level Forensics and CNA programs in the CTE track; and (5) some combination of these mechanisms.

We witnessed clear examples of course, course content, and programmatic erosion over the period of our three-year ethnographic study, and each constituted a mechanism through which the original vision of high-level STEM schools and enhanced course offerings in math and science at both STEM-focused and comprehensive schools was fundamentally compromised. While this happened to some extent in Denver as well, erosion characterized Buffalo to a far greater extent than was the case in our Denver schools. As we will see in chapters 6 and 7, this had short- and long-term consequences for students' future possibilities and outcomes.

LOW PASS RATES IN BUFFALO

Similar to the situation in Denver as described in chapter 2, the erosion of math and science course offerings, programs, and course content can, in part, be explained by the fact that individual schools and the larger school district had to address two sets of interrelated accountability demands: they had to work to stay off New York State's PLA list, and they had to work to raise graduation rates. Currently in New York State, students must pass a minimum of one Regents math course and one Regents science course, including passing the accompanying Regents examination in each case, with a score of 65 or better in order to graduate from high school. In addition, students must accumulate sufficient course credits in math and science to graduate. Students need to pass three years of mathematics and three years of science in New York State (with at least one of those years being a Regents course and examination in each subject).

In table 3.1, data on New York State Regents examination scores in math and science, over a three-year period from 2010 to 2013, show that many students at the Buffalo schools in our sample had difficulty achieving a passing score or better on two foundational Regents courses in math and science: Integrated Algebra and Living Environment (formerly Biology).

As pass rates contribute to the PLA designation and to graduation rates, low pass rates have serious consequences for students as well as the school, potentially resulting in the dissolution and restructuring of schools that do not show significant progress on these measures. In an effort to ensure that as many students as possible passed at least one Regents exam in math and one in science, the schools in our Buffalo sample stopped offering a broad range of higher-level Regents courses in math and science and concentrated instead on lower-level Regents courses in hopes that more students would pass them. They simultaneously offered a wider range of non-Regents math and science courses in hopes that more students would accumulate the necessary math and science course credits to graduate. These moves also resulted in the elimination of AP math offerings and mathematized AP science offerings such as Chemistry and Physics at the Buffalo schools in our study.

Eliminating AP math courses and mathematized AP science courses while scaling back Regents offerings served two main purposes: (1) schools could target their efforts toward preparing students to pass the required *one* Regents examination in math and *one* Regents examination in science, thereby meeting state standards for graduation and

TABLE 3.1 Percentage of students scoring 55% or above, 65% or above, and 85% or above on Regents examinations, by type, at Buffalo schools, 2010–2013

	2010–2011				2011–2012				2012–2013			
	Total # tested	55%	65%	85%	Total # tested	55%	65%	85%	Total # tested	55%	65%	85%
Broadway Science Academy												
Living Environment (Biology)	234	60%	42%	0%	180	62%	38%	0%	165	56%	33%	1%
Integrated Algebra	239	50%	25%	0%	201	66%	30%	0%	187	60%	29%	0%
STEM Academy												
Living Environment (Biology)	77	77%	58%	1%	79	54%	29%	0%	137	62%	37%	0%
Integrated Algebra	100	69%	55%	0%	94	55%	24%	0%	113	65%	43%	0%
Global Horizons												
Living Environment (Biology)	81	58%	42%	0%	98	46%	22%	1%	118	56%	36%	3%
Integrated Algebra	123	45%	27%	1%	146	48%	18%	0%	157	62%	31%	3%
Lincoln												
Living Environment (Biology)	216	79%	61%	3%	168	75%	51%	4%	164	66%	38%	1%
Integrated Algebra	324	64%	41%	0%	245	78%	50%	0%	193	78%	60%	1%

Source: Data retrieved from http://data.nysed.gov/.

staying off the PLA list; and (2) schools could consolidate their human resources into non-Regents courses aimed at students accumulating sufficient credits to graduate. While these moves may accomplish the task of raising graduation rates and staying off the PLA list, these erosions simultaneously undermined the original vision of offering more high-level math and science courses at both STEM-focused and traditional comprehensive schools in Buffalo.

As state tests differ markedly both in content and with regard to what constitutes "proficiency," we could not compare proficiency rates between Buffalo and Denver or conduct detailed analyses of test score data over time. It is clear, however, that proficiency rates in Buffalo were low in core STEM subjects and that attending a STEM-focused school did not noticeably raise rates of proficiency in science or math. As table 3.1 shows, 0 percent to 4 percent of students consistently scored at the 85% "mastery" level (the standard in New York) in math across the four sampled schools over the three-year period, and 18 percent to 61 percent scored at the "passing" level in math. In science, Lincoln (comprehensive) ranked highest, with 4 percent of students scoring 85% or better in science in 2012. In this same school, only 51 percent obtained even a passing score in science in 2012. At STEM Academy (STEM focused), only 1 percent of students obtained "mastery," and only in 2010–2011, and only on the Living Environment (science) exam, over the three-year period represented in the table.

In light of these data, STEM Academy and Broadway Science had perhaps understandably moved to raise overall test performance by eliminating high-level math and science courses. It is also arguably the case that school personnel genuinely wanted to ensure that as many low-income and minoritized students graduated from high school as possible, and that less demanding courses, particularly in math and science, would enable this to happen. Unfortunately, this collective set of moves fundamentally compromised initially envisioned enhanced opportunity structures for STEM, limiting future options with regard to STEM in college and career. We see this clearly in chapter 6 where we compare post-high school outcome data across schools and cities.

"SHADOW CAPITAL" IN BUFFALO

It is commonplace in sociological research in education to draw on Pierre Bourdieu's concept of "capital."[10] For Bourdieu, *capital* refers to anything that can be used in the production of social mobility or the maintenance of individual or group privilege. Bourdieu divided capital into three types: economic, social, and cultural. Economic capital consists of monetary resources that can be used to improve one's standing in the social hierarchy. Certain financial investments in education, for example, may produce returns in the form of access to highly ranked colleges or well-paying jobs, thereby leading to increased social standing.[11] However, not all financial investments lead to higher status. Financial investments must be well placed with respect to the existing social hierarchy if they are to contribute to social mobility. For example, in the United States today, financial capital invested in a STEM degree is likely to generate higher lifetime economic and social returns than a similar investment in an education degree.[12]

The same mechanisms apply to social and cultural capital. Social capital refers to interpersonal resources (relationships and networks) that can be used to attain social mobility or reproduce high socioeconomic standing. For example, William Julius Wilson argued that residents concentrated in high-poverty urban neighborhoods—what he called "the truly disadvantaged"—were more likely to be cut off from certain social networks, such as those that could facilitate access to better schools or provide job leads that could increase the chances of social mobility.[13] Thus, investments in social networks, as defined earlier, made by residents in high-poverty areas were unlikely to produce the same returns as similar investments in social networks in more affluent neighborhoods.

Bourdieu's concept of cultural capital is arguably most relevant to the study we discuss in this book. Cultural capital consists of knowledge, norms, and understandings that enable individuals or groups to sustain or improve their social standing. In this sense, the kind of math or science knowledge acquired in high school STEM courses is a form of cultural capital that *can* be "exchanged"—under the right circumstances—for access to higher levels of math or science (advanced courses, entrance to college STEM majors), and, in turn, improved employment opportunities and consequent social mobility. However, as is the case for economic and social investments, not all cultural investments in STEM have equivalent "exchange value." That is, some forms of so-called STEM knowledge, norms, and understandings, although well intended and well learned, have relatively little exchange value in the subsequent academic and occupational marketplace. This is the case for what Kristin Cipollone and Amy Stich call "shadow capital"—a form of cultural capital that has relatively little exchange value moving forward.[14]

Cipollone and Stich, drawing on data from STEM Academy and Broadway Science, argued that these Buffalo schools produced "shadow" rather than "dominant" STEM capital. By this they meant that while the schools promised and touted advanced STEM coursework and programs leading to four-year colleges and STEM professions (high-level STEM capital), they did not deliver on this promise. Instead, the schools continued to imply that high-level STEM capital was available when in fact it really was not, as advanced STEM coursework and four-year college-bound programming were scaled back or eliminated. This was particularly clear at Broadway Science, where initially offered high-status STEM capital intended to position students for entrance into a Research I university in biopharmaceutical sciences was eroded and replaced with capital that provided access only to more vocational, low-wage STEM pathways. In fact, as noted by Cipollone, Stich, and Weis, "Students are provided access to more vocational, low-wage STEM pathways under the impression that such pathways will allow them to actualize their goals of becoming doctors and surgeons."[15] This "bait and switch" left students with little to no dominant STEM capital in the form of high-level math and science preparation, opportunities to work with STEM mentors, or instrumental school experiences in STEM that could be exchanged for entrance into competitive four-year postsecondary institutions and high-level STEM majors in college. Cipollone, Stich, and Weis call out the deceptive nature of shadow capital when they write: "As a unique form of cultural capital, shadow capital contains a great deal of power in its ability to deceive. It arises out of good intentions to increase access to dominant knowledge, skills, and material and discursive conditions, but . . . strained from it are its most valuable component parts before it is consumed by those who are, at least initially, unaware of its transformation."[16]

While the intent to make dominant STEM capital increasingly available to low-income and minoritized students in Buffalo was laudable, its goal was quickly compromised, as available STEM capital became a *shadow* of its intended form, with less and less utility or "cachet" in dominant spaces moving forward.

Importantly, we did not find shadow capital to the same extent in Denver, at least not for the high-achieving students who comprised our focal group. In Denver, some promised increases in STEM courses and advanced STEM courses did occur and were sustained over the course of our study. These courses were also taken in sequence to scaffold developing knowledge and skills. Although the academy programming did not succeed, students continued to have greater access to higher-level STEM coursework, and focal students continued to take this STEM coursework to a far greater extent than was the case in Buffalo. We return to these issues and this comparison between the schools in the two cities in subsequent chapters.

LOST OPPORTUNITIES

In spite of the uniformly expressed desire to markedly expand STEM opportunities for minoritized students through the establishment of inclusive STEM-focused schools and some initial and authentic enhancements to STEM offerings in comprehensive schools, at the end of our three-year ethnographic investigation the situation in the Buffalo schools was markedly worse, not better. The Biopharmacy program was disbanded at Broadway Science after five years of operation, while the two CTE programs, HOT and Forensics, were expanded, thereby reducing options for advanced math/science courses in high school and for later college and career options for top students. The Forensics program at Broadway Science lacked a science component and was disconnected from both the math and science departments, again limiting college and career options in STEM. The initially offered array of AP and Regents math and science courses was also severely eroded. Course content was diminished within some existing math and science courses, with the collective consequence that intended large-scale expansion of dominant STEM capital, *via a substantially expanded opportunity structure for STEM*, was replaced with an elusive array of "shadow STEM capital." In consequence, future opportunities in STEM in college and career, as initially envisioned in these schools, were severely eroded.

In neither city was the enthusiasm and intention to reform STEM education by establishing STEM-focused schools fully realized. As we suggest in chapter 1, in Denver there was strong public support for the idea of STEM-focused schools in general and the career academy model in particular. At the time our study began, the two Denver STEM-focused schools were newly formed and newly reorganized as career academy schools. As part of this reform, increases in math and science courses were planned, and the proportion of advanced math and science courses rose. But, as in Buffalo, these good intentions quickly collided with other requirements of schooling. Graduation requirements, accountability demands, and students' weak academic performance worked against plans to offer, enroll, and staff the number and array of advanced STEM courses that were promised. In Denver, as in Buffalo, these competing factors contributed to the cancellation of some advanced math and science course offerings and the rapid collapse of the academy structure, including the anticipated opportunity to emphasize STEM in high school coursework. These instances of erosion, the mechanisms through which such erosion was accomplished, and their implications for students' pursuit of STEM in college and career were made especially clear in the case of the Buffalo schools described in this chapter. As we argue in chapter 6, focal student transcripts from the four years of high school make clear that the erosion of advanced math and science courses (defined in chapter 6 as AP and International Baccalaureate [IB] STEM courses completed) was *notably deeper* in Buffalo than in Denver, contributing to differential outcomes among similarly capitalized minoritized students in the sample schools in the two cities.

The dissolution of high-level math courses—key forms of highly valued and exchangeable sets of capital in the academic marketplace—in the two cities was particularly problematic with respect to opportunities for postsecondary options and higher-level STEM careers, because successful completion of high-level math courses such as Algebra II/Trigonometry (and increasingly, Pre-calculus) is a strong predictor of admission to highly competitive colleges.[17] Additionally, as knowledge of mathematics scaffolds critically important science courses, such as mathematized courses in chemistry and physics, the fact that students do not possess competence in higher-level mathematics means they are not prepared for courses that are necessary for higher-level postsecondary STEM majors and higher-level STEM careers.[18] This was particularly problematic in Buffalo, as shown in this chapter.

When Broadway Science closed its Biopharmacy program and funneled high-achieving math and science students into a CTE program for CNAs, it completely shut down options for higher-level preparation for a STEM career in favor of preparation for low-wage, entry-level labor. When the originally conceived Forensics program at Broadway Science backed away from its intent to focus on forensic science and focused instead on issues of general law enforcement, it limited the opportunity for students to pursue scientifically based forensic science in college and career. As a consequence, the Forensics program at Broadway Science—a dedicated STEM school under the reform effort—functioned *in the guise of STEM*, becoming a STEM program *in name only*. These moves collectively contradicted the original vision and early enactment of inclusive STEM-focused schools and limited, rather than expanded, opportunities to pursue STEM, especially higher-level STEM.

Although "reform fever" characterizes much change that is taking place in US schools, the recent focus on reforming education in STEM offers particularly promising possibilities, as, unlike some other contemporary school reform efforts, it attempts to address the problem of equalizing opportunities by focusing on enhancement of the opportunity structure itself. However, as Sharon Lynch and colleagues note (referring specifically to inclusive STEM schools), the results of this effort are as yet unclear.[19]

Findings presented in this chapter and the preceding one offer a cautionary tale with regard to the successful implementation of recent STEM school reform by means of planned augmentation of the school opportunity structure. Our study illuminates the ways in which attempts to enhance curricular opportunities for STEM—including marked expansion of dominant STEM capital—can be quickly eroded, unraveled, compromised, and redirected toward less promising ends. Importantly, these ends were increasingly divorced from the original intent of the inclusive STEM school movement and the original intent in each city. As we show here, this is particularly evident in Buffalo, where planned dominant STEM capital was quickly eradicated in favor of shadow STEM capital—with notably less exchange value in the educational and occupational marketplace.

CHAPTER 4

Diverting and Outsourcing College and STEM Counseling

"[It] has become increasingly apparent that school counselors need to increase their awareness of twenty-first century career opportunities, particularly STEM-relevant information . . . [School] counselors have the opportunity to bring together teachers and administrators to create an opportunity for [STEM] career awareness for school personnel, students, and their families."[1]

High school guidance counselors are known to play important roles in preparing young people for postsecondary education and careers. In their article on the role they should play in STEM academic and career planning, Schmidt and colleagues note that high school counselors "function on the front lines of career awareness and help the current generation explore the world of work."[2] They introduce students to postsecondary options, help them explore the possibilities at assorted colleges, assist them in preparing college and job applications, and alert them to opportunities for financial aid. Especially for students whose family members have not attended college or who have little knowledge of the complexities of college admission, high school counselors are valuable advisors and mentors for young people approaching high school graduation.[3]

Proponents of successful inclusive STEM-focused high schools include strong mentoring and college and career guidance counseling programs in their list of key components of these schools.[4] Yet, in a 2010 study, Schmidt and colleagues found that school counselors had little time to advise students about career options and "focused less on mathematics and science career opportunities than those of other subject areas."[5] Research additionally suggests that the role of school counseling is rapidly changing in the twenty-first century, as technological developments influence employment opportunities for high school and college graduates. Schmidt's team argued that high school counselors need special training to create connections between STEM classroom experiences and future careers, and they should learn more about STEM career options and trends, deliberately emphasize career options in STEM, and encourage students, including underrepresented students, to take challenging math and science courses in high school.[6]

In this chapter, we look at college and career counseling, first in Buffalo and then in Denver.[7] We examine the counseling departments, the college and career resources available for counselors and students, and the support available for students to take high-level STEM courses and consider STEM futures.

The counseling data from Buffalo discussed in this chapter were collected in two public high schools: Broadway Science, one of the STEM-focused schools that was part of our larger study (80 percent free or reduced lunch [FRL], 97 percent underrepresented minorities); and Forestview, a comprehensive suburban high school that was not part of this study as it served a group of students who were largely, but not entirely, middle/upper middle class and White (10 percent FRL; 9 percent underrepresented). The inclusion of Forestview in this chapter allows us to consider differences in counseling contexts in schools that serve non-privileged and privileged students in public high schools in adjacent districts.

We also include data from one of the Denver schools in this study, Chavez High. Like Broadway Science, Chavez was a STEM-focused school serving non-privileged, mostly underrepresented students (74 percent FRL; 85 percent underrepresented).

BROADWAY SCIENCE AND FORESTVIEW IN BUFFALO

Broadway Science is located in a racially and economically segregated inner city. Not only were schools in the district segregated from their suburban neighbors, they were also part of a hierarchy of within-district segregation wherein academic criteria-based schools and charter schools separated students from relatively highly capitalized families from students in all remaining public schools within the district. Broadway Science was designated a "STEM-focused" school by the district in 2005.

In contrast, Forestview is located in a suburb with a booming local business economy and a much more privileged population. Also in contrast to Broadway Science, where the majority of students were clustered in grades 9 and 10, suggestive of high dropout rates after tenth grade, the students who attended Forestview were generally equally spread throughout each of the grades, with student enrollment increasing slightly between ninth and twelfth grades. In contrast to Broadway Science, Forestview offered a large number of honors and AP courses, including a broad range of high-level courses in math and science.

Counseling at Broadway Science

Upon entering the counseling suite at Broadway Science, one is struck by the seemingly constant stream of students walking in and out of the counselors' offices. Students fill the chairs in the open area, talking, laughing, or eating. Several students keep their food and drinks cold in the suite's private refrigerator. The counseling suite is a comfortable social space for students; they can hang out in the suite and in the adjacent College and Career Center, a small meeting room with several computers and a sparse scattering of materials on colleges and the college application process. While the counseling space is attractive to students, counselors note that the actual work of the space is not well supported. One of the Broadway counselors told us:

> We definitely need an assistant down here, at least just to sign kids in and direct them where to go, help with paperwork, filing. We don't have anybody to help with that . . . We need someone in here all the time . . . consistent so that we can have someone also helping with [student grade] transcripts and administrative work. We have all that piling up, and we are *counselors*, so we want to be there doing counseling (emphasis ours).

On any given day at Broadway Science, school counselors can be found participating in a wide range of activities, including completing state accountability paperwork, attending meetings related to student progress and discipline, monitoring or adjusting student schedules, meeting with students in crisis, running a teen pregnancy support group, attending district trainings on school safety and new technologies, and monitoring the halls during security lockdowns. There is no typical day in the life of a high school counselor at Broadway, as potential tasks associated with the job are extremely varied and often involve responding to immediate needs and emergencies. Counselors rarely know how they will be spending their time, even on a day-to-day basis. Another Broadway counselor noted:

> That is another thing: counselors don't require substitutes [as do regular classroom teachers], so we are taken out for a lot of trainings. We have Safe and Civil Schools [a district-wide committee] that we go to. We were taken out for all the SST trainings, which is the Student Support Team.[8] We are taken out for [all these] different trainings . . . They keep taking us out [rather than letting us focus on our counseling].

At the time of our study, each counselor at Broadway was responsible for the schedules, paperwork, and college preparation materials of 200 students annually, and each of these students had a variety of needs, requiring notable amounts of paperwork. A third Broadway counselor told us:

> We get bogged down with a lot of the paperwork. I would say probably on any given day, probably about 50 percent of our time [is spent doing paperwork]. Then in addition to that, now a lot of our time I think we are data entry clerks with the computer system. And that gets real frustrating.

Counselors reported feeling buried under a seemingly never-ending pile of paperwork and data entry. A major source were federal accountability requirements of No Child Left Behind/Race to the Top (NCLB/ RTTT) legislation, whereby schools were evaluated by the percentages of students who met (or failed to meet) minimum standards of performance on standardized examinations and requirements for graduation. Broadway Science, deemed PLA under RTTT, had to improve the percentage of students reaching the minimum standards in order to remain open and intact.

This collective set of demands meant there was limited time left for counseling activities, especially for high-achieving students. With far too little time available to respond to myriad needs, counselors prioritized students who were struggling in school or in personal crisis. For the most part, these students did not include high performers such as our focal students.

Counseling at Forestview

The counseling suite at Forestview had a very different climate than the one at Broadway Science. While Broadway Science lacked appropriate administrative staff, Forestview had it in abundance. Two dedicated departmental secretaries—one full time and one part time—were positioned at the entrance to the counseling suite, blocking from access anyone without an appointment or explicit permission to enter. Carefully marked work bins were located on each secretary's desk, with labels such as "Working Papers" and "Transcript Requests." Unlike at Broadway Science, where each counselor was individually responsible for a wide array of disparate tasks, including paperwork tied to state and federal accountability measures, counselors at Forestview were not responsible for such paperwork, as strictly administrative functions were handled directly by the administrative support staff. An additional administrative support person at Forestview was housed in the Counseling and Career Center located directly across the hall, bringing the number of support staff to three. Also unlike the counseling suite at Broadway, the Counseling and Career Center at Forestview was filled with extensive materials on colleges and careers, and a designated staff member was available to help students search for colleges, scholarships, and other college-related information. A Forestview counselor's description of her work context was markedly different from that detailed by counselors at Broadway:

> We have three secretaries [who] do grade reporting; they help with the master schedule; they schedule all of our appointments; they file the kids as they come in; they take parent phone calls, set up appointments with parents for us . . . They have many more things they do than that, but those are the things off the top of my head right now. We [also] do working papers here in our career center. Melanie, she's our secretary, and she does those. They do all of our college application transcripts, things like that. They [the secretaries] get the transcripts and everything ready [for submission of the dossier to colleges]. And they also maintain all of the [locked] file folders over there [pointing to a well-organized private space in the counseling suite]. They update all of the students' information when things come in.

In sharp contrast to Broadway Science, counselors at Forestview had three full-time staff members dedicated to the work of guidance and counseling. While each counselor was assigned 215 students, they dealt with a tiny fraction of the personal and family student problems and academic emergencies that characterized counselors' work at Broadway Science. They also had a robust staff to deal with much of the administration work of the office, taking this work off the shoulders of the counselors themselves. In spite of this relative abundance of resources, however, Forestview counselors similarly offered limited resources to high performing students who were interested in pursuing STEM. We will return to this issue later in this chapter. We now turn to an analysis of course scheduling and selection, one component of a high school counselor's work.

Teacher Assignment and Course Scheduling at Broadway Science and Forestview

Clearly the courses that students are assigned to take influence what they learn, as does the sequence in which the courses are scheduled and taken. This was a problem at Broadway Science. The teachers there often did not know which science courses they would be teaching until the first day of the school year. At an early point in our study, a researcher asked a teacher:

> RESEARCHER: When did you find out you would be teaching chemistry this year?
>
> CHEMISTRY TEACHER: Right before the start of the school year . . . I was proctoring some exams in summer school, and that is when I found out. Now, had I not been proctoring, I would have found out for sure, you know, *the day before school started* [emphasis ours].
>
> RESEARCHER: [Earlier you told me that] last year you were teaching Living Environment [a biology course]—which is a different course altogether.
>
> CHEMISTRY TEACHER: Right, which I found out [about] when I was proctoring exams [during summer school in August] the year before. You know, "give me a little heads-up."

Such short notice does not allow teachers time over the summer to prepare their courses and order materials in advance of the start of the school year. Course offerings fluctuated because sometimes there were not enough students interested or able to take challenging math and science courses, and last-minute cancellations of programs such as Biopharmacy meant redirections to other programs such as Forensics and HOT (see chapter 3). As a result, teachers more often than not spent the first few weeks of class preparing for the rest of the year. Consequently, teachers could be developing lesson plans, and students could be waiting for course materials to arrive for a month or more, resulting in a delayed start to instruction that was rarely made up during the school year.[9]

Another problem at Broadway Science was students who "fell through the cracks" in the course scheduling process. Counselors at Broadway Science admitted they did not have time to review every student's class schedule. Similarly, neither students nor parents were routinely consulted about course scheduling. Rather, schedules were "handed to them," and students took "whatever is on there." Even top-performing students could be disadvantaged in this context, as was evident when an interviewer asked Maria, a focal student in the Bio-pharmacy program at Broadway Science, the following questions:

> RESEARCHER: So, last year [sophomore year/grade 10] you had Physiology, and you weren't in a science this year. But you were in the Biopharmacy program?
> MARIA: YES.
> RESEARCHER: Are you still in that?
> MARIA: I don't know.

Maria's admission that she "does not know" whether she is still in the flagship Biopharmacy program in grade 11 was stunning. Three weeks into her junior year/grade 11, we received Maria's course schedule in order to set up classroom observations. At that time, we realized Maria had not been scheduled into a *single* science course. This occurred despite a state requirement that she complete three years of science in order to graduate and the fact that Maria entered a STEM-focused school which promoted itself as preparing students for four-year colleges and STEM.

We immediately brought this oversight to the attention of one of the Broadway counselors. The counselor stated that she "forgot" to schedule Maria into a science course. She called Maria out of her math class to meet with her about the missing science course. During the meeting, Maria acknowledged she realized she was missing a science class but stated she just assumed "it was how her schedule was supposed to be" as her courses had "always been chosen for her." Needless to say, the absence of a science course during her junior year in a program dedicated to producing students for postsecondary STEM would have been a serious problem for college admission to a STEM field.

The situation at Forestview was very different. Teacher schedules were distributed during the previous school year for the following fall, and only rarely were changes made in either course offerings or teacher assignments. Such predictability in matters related to scheduling allowed teachers to have plans and materials ready when classes began.

In fact, many Forestview teachers used their ten weeks of summer vacation to prepare new lesson plans or update old plans and read about innovations in their teaching subjects.

Forestview students and parents were directly involved in course scheduling, although obviously constrained by what the school offered, which in this case included a wide range of challenging math and science courses, including AP Calculus, AP Physics, AP Computer Science, and AP Chemistry. Unlike Broadway Science, where course schedules were simply handed to students, students at Forestview took an active role in soliciting instructor approval to take advanced and elective courses, and parents had to sign off on course schedules before they were submitted to counselors for final approval. Cases like Maria's were very unlikely at Forestview.

Limited Attention to Top Students, College, or STEM

Beyond providing an impressive number of advanced-level courses in math and science at Forestview, neither Broadway Science nor Forestview paid much attention to helping students prepare for STEM in college or career. While Forestview offered an array of advanced math and science courses and had roadblocks in place that ensured that students were scaffolded for success in such courses (e.g., ensuring successful completion of high-level mathematics courses before embarking on AP mathematized science courses such as AP Chemistry and AP Physics), there was little explicit counseling for college STEM entrance or careers, beyond issues related to course-taking. At both Broadway Science and Forestview, we found that counselors paid little if any attention to college or career planning in STEM. This could have profound consequences for college and career preparation for top students who were interested in STEM, were likely to go to college, and did not have college-savvy family members to assist them. Broadway Science student Jasmine commented on her interactions with her guidance counselor:

> JASMINE: I talk to my guidance counselor [about colleges], but she just keeps saying that I have to wait until I become a senior to really look into it. But I don't want to wait until I become a

senior, and then I be running around trying to do everything, trying to hand in everything. I want to do some stuff now, so it won't be so hard.

RESEARCHER: Has anyone at home talked to you about college?

JASMINE: Well, my home life, probably my godfather, he help me a lot 'cause he been [to college]—nobody in my family really been to college, so they can't really tell me about nothing that they never been to. But my godfather, he went, and he telling me, like, "Make sure you do this, do that, talk to your counselor." And I keep telling him that I can't, because she [the counselor] won't help me.

Jasmine wanted to start searching for colleges, applying for financial aid, and looking for scholarships during her junior year of high school, but her counselors were not able to help her given demands on their time that they found more pressing. The counselors at Broadway admitted they did not have the time to work with juniors who were not in crisis or in danger of not graduating. While students at Forestview met with counselors to plan for college in tenth grade or even before, and had parents who often could position their children for competitive colleges and STEM careers, students like Jasmine at Broadway Science were told to wait until their senior year to even talk with a counselor about college preparation.

Some Broadway Science students received some college and career exposure through the HOT program at the school (discussed in chapter 3), but other students were on their own. One such student was Kobi, who was asked by a researcher:

RESEARCHER: Does the school ever talk to you about college? Do you go to any college fairs or trips or anything?

KOBI: No. I know [some] juniors who are doing it [college prep], but I never got chosen for that.

RESEARCHER: Would you like to do that?

KOBI: Yes.

A student like Kobi, who would be the first in his family to graduate high school, would have greatly benefited from college fairs, campus visits, or even simple conversations with his counselors about the college process. The interviewer continued:

RESEARCHER: What do you think that colleges look for in applicants?

KOBI: I guess three or more years of a definite [sic] language.

RESEARCHER: OK. So, [they look for a] foreign language. What other kind of stuff?

KOBI: Penmanship?

RESEARCHER: OK. Sounds like you are not really sure.

KOBI: Yeah, I have never really filled out a college application.

Kobi's responses make clear that he lacked basic information about the college preparation process and about what colleges might be looking for in selecting students. Many top-performing students at Broadway Science, like Kobi, struggled with limited and even erroneous information about colleges, the college application process, and desired STEM careers. Kobi did not know that penmanship is not a criterion for admission, nor did he realize that applications were completed almost entirely online, where penmanship is wholly irrelevant. One researcher also noted in her field notes serious misunderstandings with regard to Scholastic Aptitude Test (SAT) scores:

The students that were interviewed today appear to have a misunderstanding of how SAT scores are interpreted. While most colleges list their range of SAT scores as a total of math and English combined, Broadway students were speaking in terms of their scores as a total of *all three* sections: math, English, and the written essay portion. This would not be problematic if the students understood the difference between their scores and the averages listed on the websites of the colleges of their choice. However, the students did not understand this difference and were talking about themselves as having scored within an acceptable range to attend the schools of their choice. Meanwhile, their scores are several hundred points below the minimum for entrance to those schools.

Despite the fact that Broadway Science was a district-designated STEM-focused school, the school offered very little counseling for college preparation or admission and no counselor-driven focus on connecting students to postsecondary STEM majors and programs.

COUNSELING AT CHAVEZ HIGH SCHOOL IN DENVER

There were striking similarities between Chavez, one of the two STEM-focused schools in Denver, and Broadway Science in Buffalo.[10] There were also some differences. Both schools experienced large-scale shifts in programs and staff during the five years preceding the start of our study. At both schools, changes were driven primarily by pressure to increase academic performance (based on standardized test scores) in line with state and federal accountability measures and punishments (principal firings, teacher turnover, and program restructuring) meted out if achievement scores did not improve. Guidance counselors at both schools were charged with course scheduling and monitoring the progress of low performing students, leaving little time for college or career counseling, particularly for high-achieving students. An important difference was the availability of college-linking programs at Chavez but not at Broadway. College-linking programs, often in partnership with external sponsors, provided resources to facilitate the transition from high school to college.[11] These programs filled some of the college counseling gap for many of the focal students at Chavez.

At the time of our study, Chavez was designated a "Priority Improvement" school under Colorado's school performance framework and was therefore operating with a "school improvement plan," specifying that unless certain academic goals were met within three years, the school would be reorganized (again) (see chapter 2). Enhancements at Chavez under the improvement plan included the new academy structure and additional math and science courses, but as was the case at Broadway Science, actual opportunities fell short of expectations, many course scheduling problems ensued, and the counselors at Chavez spent the majority of their time on scheduling and tracking students at risk of not graduating.

As described in chapter 2, Chavez was a new school built in 2009 to replace an aging building and to accommodate the new academy structure, including a Science and Technology Academy. During its first year, the academy structure seemed to work in the sense that the majority of students took all their classes in their assigned academy. However, by the second year, the school began to attract more students, and counselors had trouble scheduling enough classes for each academy. Counselors directed students into classes wherever space was available. Thus, a student choosing the Science and Technology Academy might be placed in an algebra class in the Liberal Arts Academy where class sizes for algebra were smaller. And because there were few students qualified or interested in taking advanced math courses such as Precalculus and Calculus in the Science and Technology Academy, those classes were canceled. In addition, the International Baccalaureate (IB) program at Chavez was discontinued in 2011 on the grounds that no one had earned an IB diploma in three years, at least in part because too few IB classes were offered to meet the requirements for an IB diploma. Thus, course availability at Chavez was in flux every semester, and counselors spent most of their time scheduling and rescheduling students into classes on a space-available basis and closely monitoring student progress toward high school graduation.

Counseling and Course Scheduling at Chavez

Counselors at Chavez had an even higher caseload than those at Broadway Science—an average of 470 students per counselor—and the structure of the counseling program changed every year of our study. The first arrangement (the 2010–11 academic year) found counselors assigned to students for two years (e.g., their freshman and sophomore years). Then for one year (2011–12) counselors were assigned by academy. The third year (2012–13), as the academy system was breaking down, counselors were assigned to students in alphabetical order.

By their senior year, most of the high-achieving focal students in our study had had three different counselors, none of whom knew the students well. During students' senior year, the counselors were required to communicate in person with every student who was in danger of not graduating, to send letters home to their parents, and to document communication with the family. About this, one counselor said, "It's really time intensive . . . I just printed their first-semester transcripts [glances at a large pile on her desk], and now I am going through them, and it's probably going to take me a couple of weeks to hunt down all the kids that failed something that they need in order to graduate." Thus, similar to Broadway Science, students who were not on track to graduate, of which there were many at Chavez, received lots of attention from the counselors while top-performing students received very little.

The scheduling and graduation monitoring demands placed on counselors at Chavez caused them to nearly abandon the high performing students at the school. In fact, students who were on track to graduate were left entirely on their own to select their classes for senior year, not unlike the situation at Broadway Science. As a result, the students decided, not unreasonably perhaps, that they could take whatever they wanted to take. Most of the high-achieving focal students in our study enrolled in "fun" (non-college prep) classes, hoping for an "easy year" and a higher GPA. For many, this meant not taking science or math in their senior year. Without advice from counselors or others, the students were unaware that four years of high school math and science are often required for admission to a four-year college even though they were not required for high school graduation in their particular school district. Students interested in STEM fields were especially disadvantaged when advanced science or math courses were not offered because so few students were eligible or interested in taking them.

As at Broadway Science, students aspiring to attend college had to take the initiative to plan for college because their counselors did not have time to assist them. At both Broadway Science and Chavez, the majority of such students did not have family or community members who could offer help or advice. One counselor told us, "It breaks my heart every day because I know without it [college advising], any kid, but especially kids in this population, need the push all the time." Another counselor told us that this situation was quite different from only five years ago (before the academy structure and the attendant enrollment increase), when there were twice as many counselors for half as many students. At that time, she had been able to meet with students individually to talk about college and other post-high school plans. She felt terrible that she could no longer do that but said she had no choice in the matter: as at Broadway Science, much of her time was devoted to working with students who might not graduate from high school.

When students at Chavez became seniors, the counselors did pay some attention to those who wanted to attend college. But they did so in whole-class or whole-grade-level meetings held only infrequently. These meetings occurred only twice during our focal students' senior year, and there was no opportunity for students to meet individually with a counselor for college planning. When asked about college readiness among seniors (in 2012–13), one Chavez counselor said, "This year we made a concentrated effort to go into every senior English class," implying that this had not been done in the past, and also implying that senior-year college counseling could only be done in large groups. Although counselors talked about the importance of parent nights to discuss topics such as scholarships, the college application process, and FAFSA® (Free Application for Federal Student Aid, the application necessary to apply for federal grants, work study, and student loans), these nights occurred only once a year, and few parents attended.

In these ways, counseling at Chavez was similar to counseling at Broadway Science in Buffalo. But unlike Broadway Science, the counselors at Chavez also "outsourced" college counseling to college-linking programs, local college representatives, homeroom teachers, and online programs. It was these arrangements, rather than the counselors themselves, that provided college counseling services and any STEM career planning at the school.

Outsourcing to College-Linking Programs

Chavez established partnerships with several admissions departments at local colleges and community colleges to provide college counseling for its students. This was a step beyond what was available at Broadway Science. One program, City Excel (pseudonym), offered by a nonselective, local university, sent two representatives once a week to work with students at Chavez to complete college and scholarship applications and the FAFSA form. About City Excel, a Chavez counselor commented, "They stay with us every Wednesday all day and just help our kids apply to college, and any kid can walk in. They target kids who usually have a 2.5 to 3.5 GPA. I will just give her all of those kids and all of their schedules, and she will just call them down, all of them, one by one throughout the year."

Given that the high school counselors were unable to provide regular college guidance counseling, City Excel provided valuable services to students at Chavez. However, although ostensibly offering guidance about various college options, City Excel used the opportunity to promote its own local university, a questionable choice for high-achieving students.

Chavez also had a connection with one of the state's selective four-year universities. A few years prior, the university had approached Chavez asking to partner in a program to recruit students from high schools with large populations of first-generation students. Chavez agreed, and university representatives came to the high school during freshman orientation. They set up a mock college dorm room in a classroom and talked about ways to prepare for college. The program also sponsored several visits to the university campus each year, and small scholarships were available for any Chavez student who was accepted at the school. One counselor told us, "I feel like we have seen an increase in the number of students who go to [the partner university] now, who have felt like it's a comfortable and welcoming . . . and supportive school, and that is really important for our students—that is really important for first-generation students to feel that way."

This program generated a lot of interest among the ninth graders who participated, but few Chavez students would eventually meet the university's criteria for admission. Only one of our focal students at Chavez attended this university.

Nationally, college-linking programs provide students with social, cultural, and economic capital to help them navigate the college search and application process. Some of these programs include courses taken during the high school day while others are outside-of-school programs. Programs like Precollegiate, Upward Bound, and Talent Search afford underrepresented students the opportunity to visit and sometimes study in the summer at four-year college campuses. Students also receive help with college applications, scholarship searches, and test preparation. A college-linking program called Advancement Via Individual Determination or AVID was offered as a regular class (with a regular assigned teacher) at Chavez every year to familiarize students with college expectations and the college application process (applications, essays, and scholarship sources).

Although Chavez offered several of these college-linking programs, most were small, offering few spots for participating students. For example, Talent Search at Chavez took four students per grade, as did Upward Bound. Based on student interviews, these programs were popular among students, and many more students wanted to participate than were able to do so.

AVID accommodated more students by offering a course each year (as an elective). The courses stressed study skills, academic support, and college exploration and preparation. Of all the college-linking programs at Chavez, AVID seemed to have made the most difference to the focal students at that school. All the Chavez focal students who pursued math or science in college participated in AVID during high school, and they spoke effusively about their AVID teachers and the college support and preparation help they provided. It is important to note that no such programs were available to comparable students in schools like Broadway Science in Buffalo.[12] Ana, a focal student at Chavez, had this to say about AVID: "We have [AVID] tutorials twice a week. We get help with classes, and we do, like, a career research project—we had to research two colleges and two careers and write a report on each. We also practiced for the ACT. My counselor sends me reminders about college [representative] visits, but it's my AVID teacher who really helps me with college."

Chavez also used what they called "homerooms with a college focus" to disseminate information about college and the application process. All students were expected to spend thirty minutes of homeroom discussing college issues each day. Freshmen were supposed to learn and practice study skills; sophomores were supposed to complete career inventories; juniors were supposed to learn about the ACT and how to write college essays; and seniors were supposed to work on college applications. All teachers were supposed to cover this material as part of their homeroom responsibilities, but no one checked on compliance. Even though the counseling department had developed a loose curriculum for this purpose, counselors, teachers, and students admitted that homeroom was mostly used as a study hall.

In the final year of our study at Chavez, the new principal mandated that all seniors apply to three community colleges—his attempt to assure that his school's measure of "students accepted to college," a state accountability indicator, would go up. Students were expected to complete these applications during homeroom. This new rule created a lot of confusion. Some teachers thought students should apply only to community colleges. Others thought they should apply to colleges they expected to get into. Some thought students should apply to one "reach" college and two "easy" colleges. Some students did not want to apply to any colleges, much less three, because they knew they could not afford to go to college or did not want to go, even to a community college. One senior told us at the beginning of the year that she had been planning to apply to four or five 4-year colleges, but by late fall, she had applied to three community colleges, because that's what she was told to do by her homeroom teacher. Another senior, Anne, a high-achieving student with hopes of attending a four-year university, told us, "Today they made us fill out community college applications— it was mandatory for every senior. All the people who want to go to a four-year university, they're not helping *us*. They're trying to raise the school's numbers [percent accepted to any college, a state accountability metric], but they're not helping us." Anne went on to complain that because of this requirement, she had "done all these applications" but not for the schools she wanted to attend. So, "I just took over the counselor's job and started doing it myself [for four-year schools]."

In the absence of critical college counseling from counselors at Chavez, college-linking programs and schoolwide mandates provided some guidance and assistance to students hoping to attend college. This is in sharp contrast to Buffalo, where students were left almost entirely on their own in a school like Broadway Science—a school comparable to Chavez. Such programs met a need that the schools' guidance counselors could not meet due to expressed higher-priority demands on their time. However, as Anne's words suggest, it is important to note that this arrangement was not necessarily appropriate or helpful for high-achieving students who aspired to go beyond the school's minimum expectations for college attendance. In addition, to our knowledge, like the situation more generally at the Buffalo schools discussed earlier in this chapter, none of these programs gave any special attention to students' STEM interests or to preparation for college majors or career pathways in STEM.

Outsourcing to Online Programs

In Denver, online programs were another form of outsourcing college support. Two programs, *Naviance* and *College in Colorado*, were highly touted by administrators as a solution to the need for more college counseling in the high schools. *Naviance* is a nationwide online platform that school districts must purchase; it is designed to help counselors, students, and parents match college preferences and expectations with postsecondary options. There are various components to the program, and each component has an added cost. The basic *Naviance* package includes career interest surveys to help students identify their interests and match them with college offerings. Add-ons include college planning activities, from basic college searches and places to sign up for college visits, to detailed statistics about an individual student's academic record and likelihood of acceptance and enrollment at various colleges.

College in Colorado is similar but is limited to the state of Colorado and was free to all Colorado high schools. It includes college and career assessments, college admission requirements, financial aid advice, and sample documents such as letters of recommendation. The Denver schools that adopted these programs (all four Denver schools in our study) anticipated that students, together with their parents, would use the technology to explore college options, prepare applications, and research future careers. In the absence of time for counselors to provide college counseling, these two online programs, in conjunction with college-linking programs, were used to fill the need. To many administrators, the online programs were considered superior to counselors and even to in-person college-linking programs because of the wealth of information about the immense variety of colleges in the United States, their various emphases, and their numerous requirements. However, students, parents, and even counselors at Chavez made very little use of these resources.

Chavez purchased only the basic *Naviance* component, and counselors occasionally used it to invite college representatives to visit the school and to obtain a list of college fairs at nearby schools. Counselors occasionally demonstrated *Naviance* during homeroom periods and encouraged students to use the program with the help of a teacher or parent. However, in our interviews with counselors, teachers, and students, *Naviance* and *College in Colorado* were seldom mentioned. When asked specifically about them, only two of the high-achieving focal students in our study reported using them for their own college searches. Several students claimed they had never heard of them.

When we asked administrators about difficulties that might arise for students and parents trying to use these programs at home (lack of an available computer, limited internet service), they claimed that students could access the programs on the school's computers during the school day. But teachers told us there was no time in their daily schedules for students to leave class to use the school's computers. Students told us they often had to share computers at home, and their first priority was completing homework, leaving little time for *Naviance* even if they wanted to use it. Some students did not have internet access at home. In effect, these online resources were not easy for Chavez students to use, and not surprisingly, they rarely used them.

· · ·

In summary, the counseling situation at Chavez was similar to that at Broadway Science in important ways. Counselors were largely diverted from college and career counseling to scheduling and reporting functions in both schools. Under Chavez's school improvement plan, the specter of harsh sanctions for low graduation rates loomed large, threatening the school's existence and leading school administrators to require counselors to prioritize low performing students who might not graduate from high school. The specter of low rates of college acceptance was also threatening, leading administrators to require every senior to apply to three community colleges regardless of other desires or choices. In this context, high performing students, including those interested in STEM fields, were left on their own to plan and schedule course-taking and to investigate other colleges and careers. In Denver, Chavez tried to make up for the lack of counseling by outsourcing these activities, including purchasing online platforms with college resources for students and parents to use. Unfortunately, many students and parents did not or were not able to access these resources. In the case of parents, many were unfamiliar with the technology as well as the overall process that comprises college admissions. While parents may have felt uncomfortable speaking with the school counselors about the college admissions process in relation to their children, in all likelihood they felt far more uncomfortable with the technology that undergirds online programs such as *Naviance* and *College in Colorado*.

STEM STUDENTS ADRIFT AS COUNSELORS ARE DIVERTED AND SERVICES OUTSOURCED

Writing about the importance of career counseling in STEM, Schmidt and colleagues had this to say: "The momentum toward STEM career planning provides ideal opportunities for school counselors to address students' career trajectories, specifically, course advisement and selection, promotion of academic rigor, strategic emphasis on achievement and goal orientation, commitment to parental inclusion, and attention to underrepresented populations."[13]

Clearly the schools we studied in Denver and Buffalo did not fulfill this promise. At both Broadway Science in Buffalo and Chavez in Denver (two STEM-focused schools), guidance counselors were consistently diverted from college and career counseling by accountability demands placed on the two schools. In these two schools, as well as the other three schools in Buffalo and two schools in Denver, counselors became course schedulers and graduation cops, charged with making sure that students were scheduled into classes that put them on track to graduate from high school rather than on track to excel in STEM or to be positioned for STEM in college or career. Counselors reported spending less than 25 percent of their time on college counseling, and then primarily for high school seniors only. This near-total repurposing of the college guidance counselor's role differed dramatically from that outlined in the preceding quote, from College Board, and from proponents of inclusive STEM-focused high schools, all of which emphasize providing tools and resources for researching colleges and professions, identifying "best-fit" colleges, facilitating college applications, and explaining financial aid.[14] In consequence, high-achieving students in both Denver and Buffalo who wanted to attend college and were considering STEM fields and careers were left largely on their own to consider and choose colleges and college majors and to position themselves in existing school courses to be qualified and ultimately competitive for the colleges and majors they chose.

The situation in Denver, though far from ideal, was somewhat better than in Buffalo. Some college-linking programs and online resources were available in Denver. We found that many of the Denver focal students participated in the available college-linking programs, and they credited these programs with providing good advice about choosing colleges and applying to colleges, and useful information about what to expect once in college. Although the programs could not accommodate all the students who wanted to participate, and some resources, though available, were not easily accessed by students or their families, the programs offered some college and career support that was not available in the Buffalo schools we studied. The difference in college and career counseling opportunities between Denver and Buffalo described in this chapter parallels the difference in course-taking opportunities between Denver and Buffalo described in chapters 2 and 3. These *accumulating differences* portend our findings about focal student outcomes in chapters 6 and 7.

Finally, it is important to note that in none of the Denver or Buffalo schools in our study was any special attention given to planning and preparing for pursuing STEM interests in college or career. The high-achieving focal students in our study schools who, for the most part, performed well in high school math and science and were interested in pursuing STEM beyond high school, did not receive any programmatic guidance or support in high school to pursue STEM. A few students had parents or other adults who could assist them, but most did not.

CHAPTER 5

Figured Worlds of Success in High School Math and Science

"Students ('smart' and 'dumb') and teachers populate the figured world of the traditional classroom in which students are concerned with completing assignments and getting 'good' (or good enough) grades. Assignments, worksheets, homework, and report cards are among the most relevant artifacts in this world."[1]

"To be a good student in this figured world called for compliance with rote, repetitive tasks that were distanced from meaning, amid humiliating interactions and unflattering categorizations . . . In this world, a 'good student' was compliant, worked quickly and alone, and did not present problems or difficulties requiring a teacher's attention. The way to tell that someone was smart, students reported, was if he or she received good grades."[2]

"[A] subject area classroom can form a figured world with the power to shape students' senses of themselves as learners of that particular subject [emphasis in original]."[3]

These quotations introduce the idea of "figured worlds," first proposed by Dorothy Holland and colleagues as a way to investigate the cultural meaning systems that develop in social settings.[4] They define a figured world as a "socially and culturally constructed realm of interpretation in which particular characters and actors are recognized, significance is assigned to certain acts, and particular outcomes are valued over others."[5] Because figured worlds are socially produced, they are defined in terms of material conditions (available artifacts, resources, and opportunities) and also discursively by people talking and acting within a context. Figured worlds mediate participants' behavior and inform their outlook.[6]

There are, of course, countless meanings that circulate in and about US schools and society, but Holland and colleagues intended to draw attention to a collection of meanings that is so prevalent as to be taken for granted and widely shared in a particular social setting such as a school. The figured world of schooling as evidenced in this chapter's opening quotations is one example. Students are not born knowing they are smart or dumb, or "good" or "not good" at math or science; they learn the meaning of these identities as they participate in social contexts.[7] In this figured world, students are discursively divided into "smart" and "dumb," "good" and "bad" according to compliance with task demands and grades. Students who behave or perform outside the parameters of the figured world can be recognized—as when a "bad" student offers a brilliant answer or a "good" student has a "bad" day—but the simplified meaning of the categorizations and divisions remains the same and both explicitly and implicitly values certain behaviors and devalues and ignores others. In this way, figured worlds "teach their participants how power works . . . In figured worlds people are ordered and ranked and power is distributed."[8] Students identified as "smart" (in this context) will be rewarded and encouraged to continue their performance and further develop a "smart" identity. These students will come to see themselves, and others will come to see them, as smart. Students recognized as "not smart" will come to see themselves, and others will come to see them, in relation to the "not smart" category. Of course, circumstances may alter a student's categorization and identity, as, for example, when a "smart" student fails to make the expected grades and thus cannot sustain a smart identity or when a "not very smart" student develops a passion for a subject area and begins to perform as a "smart" student.

Figured worlds of school math and science are constituent components of the figured world of schooling and are highly contextualized. What it means for a student to be "good" or to stand out in a positive way in math or in science can vary by school or classroom, as well as by student population, thus facilitating or interfering with access to math or science opportunities and the development of identity in STEM fields.

A few researchers have investigated the figured worlds of schooling, including the figured worlds of school science and math. Their findings are not encouraging. They repeatedly show that being a "good" math or science student, above all else, means behaving compliantly and making good grades. Jo Boaler, investigating years 8 through 11 math classrooms in six English schools representing a range of racial/ethnic and income groups, found a figured world that emphasized and rewarded narrow activities, such as following directions, repeating procedures, and copying and memorizing from textbooks and worksheets.[9] Beth Rubin, in a study of a classroom of low-income African American and Latino/a ninth graders in New Jersey, reported that "a 'good student' was compliant, worked quickly and alone, and did not present problems or difficulties requiring the teacher's attention. The way to tell that someone was smart, students reported, was if he or she received good grades." Rubin asked one student if there was anything else that could indicate that someone was smart; his response was "no."[10] While noting that some researchers have found examples of project-based classroom activities that encourage meaningful engagement in math, science, and other subjects, Rubin concluded that most classrooms are characterized by the narrow and unmotivating activities described by Boaler.[11] A decade later (2018), Katherine Wade-James and Renee Schwartz found this narrow figured world in the science classrooms of a US public all-girls' middle school composed primarily of African American girls.[12] The girls were positively recognized for being good at science when they were quiet, polite, passive, and fast workers. In this context, the girls developed a discourse of "imitation science." The authors write:

> Students who wanted to engage in [authentic] science, who liked science, had no way to gain positive recognition and, as a result engaged in a superficial imitation of what they thought science was, [including] using science vocabulary words without understanding the meaning and describing fictitious science experiences. The focus on *imitation* was seen throughout the figured world of school science, as students were positively recognized for parroting

answers to the teacher and rotely memorizing vocabulary words. Even when completing a science fair project, which seems like an obvious time to engage in [authentic] science practices, students were recognized for following specific procedures to imitate experiments found online [emphasis in original].[13]

These figured worlds discouraged students, in this case African American girls specifically, from pursuing subjects like math and science by limiting behaviors and discursive resources for developing personally meaningful identities in these subjects.[14] Importantly, they also portend difficulties when higher-order skills are needed, such as performing well on standardized tests, accessing advanced high school math and science courses, and in higher education. In these ways, figured worlds mediate the relationship between opportunity structures, individual identities and choices, and educational and occupational outcomes.

One way to investigate the figured worlds of school math and science is to listen carefully to what students and teachers say when they talk about the characteristics of students who are "good in math" or "good in science."[15] These discourses express the normative parameters for individuals wishing to be positively recognized in math or science at school. In our study in Denver, we found very similar discourses to those reported by Boaler, Rubin, and Wade-James and Schwartz, but the news was not all bad. In the four Denver schools, we found that the meaning of being good in math or science had indeed been "hollowed out"—that is, primarily conceived as procedural compliance even for high-achieving students—but there were other aspects of this figured world that were motivating.

THE FIGURED WORLD OF BEING GOOD IN MATH OR SCIENCE IN DENVER

Being "Good" in Math or Science

Focal students in Denver described a familiar figured world of schooling in which success in school was viewed as an indicator of future success in life: school was seen as a place where students were supposed to exchange obedience and work for knowledge and guidance provided by teachers.[16] "Good" students were those who adhered to procedures, obeyed their teachers, worked individually and quickly, and made good grades. The following excerpts from student interviews illustrate this orientation:

> RESEARCHER: Earlier you mentioned what it looks like to be a good student. What does it look like to be a good student?
>
> PAULA (Pella): You do what the teacher says. You get things fast. You don't take a while to understand. You don't have to depend on others.
>
> SILVIA (Southside): They receive a lot of attention from the teachers. They always get very good grades and want everything to be fine.
>
> PATRICIA (Pella) said: You have to work really, really hard, and the teacher might never tell you when the due date is, so you just have to bother the teacher until he tells you, like, when they want stuff done and *how* they want it done. It's a matter of asking *how*.
>
> ALFONSO (Chavez) agreed: They really try to be good at school and get their grades up.

Correspondingly, someone who is "really good" in math or science behaves compliantly, completes classwork quickly, and makes good grades. In addition, for those who are good in math or science, the subject comes "naturally"—the work is understood more quickly and more easily than it is by other classmates. For example, Chang (Capital) said, "People who are really good in math and science already know what's happening. They're always, like, done [with their work]. They're, like, leading the whole thing." Alma (Chavez) said that really good math students "get it" right away, without any real work or struggle. Sofia (Southside) explained that in Precalculus, she "understands everything," and she "can do all the homework on [her] own." When Alma (Chavez) was asked what made her think she was good in math, she said, "When they show us stuff, I already know it, and I know how to do it. Like, I get it really easily, and like, in other things, I take a while to learn them, and in math, I can just, like, do it really quickly." When asked about the characteristics of students who are good in math, Salvador (Southside) said, "They do good at all the math stuff; there is nothing that is hard for them."

Similar characteristics were used to describe students who are good in science. Catherine (Capital) said, "Science is a strong subject for me; it's easy for me to understand." Patricia (Pella) said about science: "It comes so easy for me, so I feel like I should just pursue that and do some sort of career with it." When a researcher asked Pedro (Pella) what made him good in chemistry, he said, "It was easy, it was easy to understand."

It is notable that the students' construction of a good student in math or science did not refer to interest, excitement, or exploration. They hardly ever mentioned being interested in the subject matter of math or science per se. There were very few comments about enjoying math or science classes or looking forward to them (one exception was science labs, but mainly to complain that there weren't enough of them). The students did not say they liked their courses because they were fascinating or informative, but because they were "easy," and the work could be accomplished quickly. Investment in effort to complete work as prescribed, do it quickly, behave properly, and make good grades were the defining features of a "good student." This is the sense in which we began to think of good-student identities in math and science as "hollowed out," or devoid of the excitement, passion, fascination, and curiosity of discovering new ideas and trying new things. Aspects of more positive figured worlds of math or science have been reported in a few studies of elementary and middle school math and science, but not to our knowledge in studies of US high schools.[17]

The high-achieving students in our study did not necessarily like these norms: they knew they paid a price for following them, namely by being called "nerds," but they considered the price essential to success in high school and the promise of college. Patricia (Pella) told us, "We are probably called nerds, like, for getting all our work done quickly, but school's my priority. It comes before sports and friends and all that stuff." Alma (Chavez) added, "I'll do it because I really, really want to go to college . . . But it's really not my thing." Here, the students anticipate the exchange value of succeeding in terms of the figured world that circulates at their schools: they will do what is expected of them in high school math or science in hopes of going to college and securing a good future.

Being "The Best People"

Somewhat perversely, there are some very positive traits associated with the impoverished meaning of being good in math or science. When Stefan (Southside) was asked what makes a good math student, he responded, "I just know that they like numbers, and it comes easy to them, too, and they're just really good. Ever since I met them, they're always the best people." Sofia (Southside) said, "They are really good people" and "it just comes naturally to them." The idea that students who do well in math or science are not just able to do the work but are also honorable—"really good people" and "the best people"—came up in several interviews. Simon (Southside) put it this way when asked about the characteristics of people who are good in math: "They're, like, very intelligent, highly intelligent. Very respectful. They're just overall good people. The best people I know." Such comments were consistent across both traditional comprehensive and STEM-focused schools in our Denver sample.

When these students talked about math or science by saying "I get it," "I'm confident," "I'm good at this," and "I can pull this off," their statements indexed more than a grade. In addition to referencing a meaning system that associates being good in math or science with the ability to grasp the subject matter easily, do the work quickly, do it without help from others, do it more quickly than others, and get an A grade, the meaning system also referenced a privileged high status (not everyone can do this) and an elevated moral standing (a better person than others). Those identified as good in math or science are "really up there," "really special," "really intelligent," "really respectful," and the "best people I know." Among the focal students' close peers, this was a positive, valued identity.

Being good at math or science was also associated with being prepared for college in a way that being good in other subject areas was not. Focal students expressed a strong desire to go to college and a belief that everyone who wanted to "be anyone" or "be successful" would want to go to college. Among Denver focal students, success in math and science (making good grades, finding it easy, and moving up the course hierarchy—for example, from Honors Algebra II to Precalculus to AP Calculus) was an indicator that a student was on track for college and, by implication, for a successful and good life.

This conjoined identity—good at math or science and ready for college—may have been especially potent because of its positive connotations across major domains of the focal students' high school lives. For this identity, teachers praised them and gave them extra attention, counselors celebrated their college plans, parents were thrilled to find their children apparently on track to a bright future, and friends admired them. This set of positive constructions around being good in math or science cut across both STEM-focused and traditional comprehensive schools in our Denver sample. However, the fact that being good in math or science, as produced in these schools, was potentially tenuous preparation for higher-level education or careers was lost in this context.

If You're Good at It, Make a Career of It

In fact, being good in math or science in these ways had formative implications for students' and their parents' thinking about colleges and careers. When Patricia (Pella) said, "I just enjoy [science] so much. It comes so easy for me, so I feel like I should just pursue that and do some sort of career with it," she was suggesting that *because* she finds it easy to do well in science, that's what she should pursue as a career. When we mentioned this to Patricia's mother, she agreed: "Yes, she just loves science, so I told her, 'I really think you should do that [as a career].'" When asked about Alma's (Chavez) career plans, her mother said, "She likes something that she knows how to do. Like, if you tell her, 'Look, this career is good; it uses mathematics,' and it's something that's easy for her, she'll want to do that." When Paloma (Pella) was asked whether she might want to major in math, she said, "I could. It's really easy for me, and I like it."

This confluence of meanings associated with being good in math or science in the Denver schools left us in a quandary. On the one hand, we were disturbed by the limited view of what makes someone a "good" math or science student and the implications for students interested in pursuing higher levels of education and careers in these fields. On the other hand, we were encouraged by the positive associations supporting those who manifested identities as "good" in these fields. Turning to Buffalo, we see that the figured world of being good in math or science was even more limiting there.[18]

THE FIGURED WORLD OF BEING GOOD IN MATH OR SCIENCE IN BUFFALO

The figured world of being good in math or science among Buffalo focal students differed from that in Denver, as did the context in which the figured world circulated. For the focal students in Denver, success in math or science (making good grades, finding it easy) was constructed in the context of moving up a sequentially ordered set of math courses from one year to the next. For example, students took Algebra I and then moved up to Algebra II/Trigonometry. They then moved on to Precalculus, often followed by Calculus. They progressed through math courses wherein one course scaffolded knowledge and success in the next course. Although this explicit course scaffolding was not set up for science courses, as high school science courses do not scaffold learning in one course to the next in the same way that mathematics courses do, most Denver focal students took an established set of science courses—Biology in tenth grade, Chemistry in eleventh, and Physics in twelfth—some of which depended in part on upper-level math skills (e.g., AP Physics). Also in Denver, focal students could and did take advanced (honors, AP, IB) courses in both math and science.

This sequencing and scaffolding did not happen in Buffalo. Focal students there were less likely to take a regular sequence of math or science courses, in large part because they struggled to pass the state Regents test requirements for high school graduation. When students had to retake courses in order to pass by Regents standards, their progress through high school was interrupted and their ability to take higher-level courses was limited. The requirement to pass Regents math and science courses and exams created a bottleneck, with large numbers of students retaking ninth- and tenth-grade math and science (Regents Living Environment, Regents Earth Science, Regents Algebra I, and Regents Geometry), leaving few eligible to take and fill eleventh- and twelfth-grade Regents or AP offerings (e.g., Regents Chemistry, Regents Physics, Regents Algebra II/Trigonometry, AP Biology, and AP Chemistry), even if such offerings were available at their school. In consequence, there were very few AP courses for even top-performing students in math and science. In three of the four Buffalo schools, there were *no* AP courses. Only STEM Academy students could take AP courses by the second year of our study, and according to teachers, these were not "real" AP courses. In fact, nearly half of STEM Academy's focal students (five out of twelve) did not take *any* math classes at all in their senior year of high school. Thus, orderly progression through math and science course content that might make higher-level courses attainable for students such as those in Denver, despite the limitations, did not occur in Buffalo. In addition, even if some Buffalo students initially stated that they found math or science "easy," the plethora of low scores on the required math and science Regents examinations quickly challenged this sense, with most students, even top students (relative to their respective schools) such as our focal students, taking the course and the exam more than once in an effort to pass with a score of 65 and be able to graduate from high school.

Our analysis of math and science course-taking patterns in Buffalo indicates that many focal students found themselves chasing Regents requirements, trying to pass at least one Regents math and one Regents science examination, over the course of their four years in high school in order to graduate. This led to an emphasis on "passing" rather than "excelling" or even "being good" in STEM courses.

"Passing" as the Standard for Success in Buffalo

Under these conditions, for the majority of focal students in Buffalo, math and science success came to mean simply passing their classes, with particular emphasis on passing the New York State math and science Regents exams with a score of 65, thereby allowing them to graduate from high school. At Broadway Science, this became clear when students talked about their grades and performance on tests:

> MARIA: Let's see . . . geometry is good now, because at first, I didn't get algebra, and then when I passed [the exam], it was so easy . . .
>
> RESEARCHER: What are your academic strengths? What do you think makes you a strong student?
>
> KENDRA: I would say math.
>
> RESEARCHER: So, is math your best subject?
>
> KENDRA: Yes.
>
> RESEARCHER: Did you do well in algebra? And you're doing well in geometry?
>
> KENDRA: Yeah, I think I got, like, a 75 on the algebra exam, the Regents.

Although Kendra stated that math was her best subject and that she did well on the algebra Regents examination, her grade of 75 on the exam is not a strong score—only ten points above passing. Her statement suggests that simply "passing," rather than excelling or distinguishing oneself in a subject, was a primary metric for "being good at math."

At Global Horizons, passing was also critical, as indicated when a researcher asked Dannika:

> RESEARCHER: Did you find Biology to be challenging or easy?
>
> DANNIKA: No, I passed Biology! [She sounded very excited about passing the course.]
>
> RESEARCHER: So, you thought it was pretty easy and you did OK?
>
> DANNIKA: I did OK.

Robert, at STEM Academy, said this about AP Biology in an interview by a researcher:

RESEARCHER: So, you just had your [AP] exam Monday?

ROBERT: Yes.

RESEARCHER: How did it go?

ROBERT: (pause) I did decent. I'm not going to [say] 'great,' because everything we studied for, they didn't emphasize.

RESEARCHER: OK, so you're not exactly sure, but you think you did OK?

ROBERT: Yeah, I got at least a 2, I know that.

RESEARCHER: A 2 is passing?

ROBERT: No, a 3 is a passing, but . . . no, 3 is like a credit, and 2, they say you get a 2 and up, it just looks good.

RESEARCHER: For college applications?

ROBERT: Yes.

Again, while Robert stated that he thinks he received "at least a 2" on the AP Biology examination, he was not correct that a 2 "looks good" for college applications. With regard to college applications, he would have to receive at least a 3 to be seen as having passed the AP exam, thereby receiving, at some schools, college course credit. Depending on where he applies to college, he would need to score a 4 or 5 to distinguish himself in the applicant pool. Where he was correct, however, is that compared to his counterparts in the STEM school he attended (STEM Academy), completing an AP class and actually *taking* the examination distinguished Robert from his immediate peers. Robert recognized the larger field within which his AP score would be judged by college admissions committees, but he misconstrued its meaning by reference to the normative expectations at his school.

Teachers at STEM Academy were aware that the AP science and math courses they offered did not cover "real" AP class content and used this rationale to explain the uniformly low scores on the exam, even among standouts like Robert, who was the valedictorian of his class. Similarly, Sadie, who was valedictorian of her senior class at Lincoln, commented on the lack of access to AP courses and talked about the closest equivalent available to her when a researcher asked whether she had taken Advanced Placement last year:

> SADIE: There was no AP available.
> RESEARCHER: No AP available, and this year? No AP?
> SADIE: No AP. The closest we have to AP is . . . the business communications. It's considered more AP, but it's more just college level. It is considered more AP because only certain students can go in there, and that's about it.

Among the Buffalo students, Sadie and Robert were the only students to state explicitly that they desired more advanced high school STEM work, and both noted a lack of AP classes. Neither student was desirous of simply "passing" as a way to distinguish themselves from other students in their high school. Nonetheless, the language of passing permeated Robert's discussion of his AP test score.

Buffalo parents in the study also stressed "passing" as a key marker of success. At Lincoln High, a parent of a focal student described her daughter as follows:

> PARENT: So, she passed her exams and her Regents and everything. So, she's a straight junior now [has all the credits needed for junior or eleventh-grade status].
> RESEARCHER: Yes, yes, she's getting closer, right? To graduating?
> PARENT: Yes, so when September comes, I'm so happy. I'm so happy.

In fact, students in this school district, who could pass any type of standardized examination, were viewed in a very positive light. They were, in the broader community parlance, considered successful, "good" students. The school counselor at Global Horizons put it this way:

> COUNSELOR: So, if you look at test scores, we've already met AYP [Adequate Yearly Progress] for the district.[19] So . . .
> RESEARCHER: That's good.

COUNSELOR: *It's fantastic.* It's 95 percent of our kids have been tested in the Regents exams that they're supposed to be tested in, and I don't know what it is, like, 85 percent have passed (with a score of 65 or above) or something like that. So, we've met AYP . . .

RESEARCHER: That's great.

COUNSELOR: *It's fantastic* (emphasis ours).

The counselor at Broadway Science offered a similar institutional perspective on passing:

We actually just had an assembly for students who *passed every single marking period* and then had good attendance; they earned prizes. And we had all these donations, so, pretty much, seventy kids were called up—the whole school was there for an assembly, and all came up at different times and got to, like, pull a gift off the board, and it ranged from, like, ten dollars and then a couple was iPads.

While we applaud Broadway Science for celebrating and rewarding students who met defined markers of success, exhibiting good attendance while passing all courses would seem to meet minimal standards rather than mark excellence. While we understand that the school, like many majority low-income institutions that serve largely minoritized students, was under pressure to meet AYP, affirming minimum expectations through the public awarding of cash prizes and an occasional iPad to seventy students for good attendance and passing courses sends a poor message. It communicates to this population that they are doing well when, in fact, they are not doing particularly well if they simply attended classes on a regular basis and passed their courses and state examinations with minimum scores. With respect to the figured worlds of math and science in Buffalo, then, the culture of *passing* constructed symbolic boundaries around the meaning of academic success as well as what comprised success for the student population attending these schools. Even Robert, STEM Academy's valedictorian, whom we might consider an exception to the predominant notion of "passing" (his average GPA hovered around 98 percent), had *learned* to be satisfied with, even proud of, a 2 on his AP exam. Although his AP exam score seemed to contradict his identity as a high-achieving student, within this particular urban space that served largely low-income and minoritized students where most students did not even take AP classes, and even fewer passed them, his score still "looked good" both within the school and within the broader family and school community.

THE NEARLY EMPTY FIGURED WORLD OF COLLEGE AND CAREER

"I Just Don't Know What They Are"

Despite high expectations for colleges and careers, many of the focal students and their parents in Denver and Buffalo lacked specific information about college admissions, enrollment, costs, scholarships, or success. They had virtually no idea what colleges require or what college life is like, even among those who achieved straight A's and liked school math or science. Students may have a label for a job they would like to have (e.g., doctor, engineer), but little more. They had no idea what a college curriculum is like, what a job for someone who loves math looks like, or what people who are engineers do. This lack of information was clear when a researcher at Chavez in Denver asked:

> RESEARCHER: So, what do you see yourself majoring in again? Once you get to college?
>
> ALMA (Chavez): I think I would probably do, having something to do with numbers, technology or something.
>
> RESEARCHER: Have you thought about computer science, or engineering, or . . .?
>
> ALMA: I think, cuz I'm not sure what's, like, all those things.
>
> RESEARCHER: It seems like engineering, physics, or math, [or] applied math is also another major you could do, and computer science is also another one.
>
> ALMA: Yeah, I've seen, like, all the different [names], but I just don't know what they are.

It was also clear when a researcher queried Antony at Chavez:

> RESEARCHER: Do you want to go to college?
> ANTONY: Yeah . . . like, I want to be . . . what is that thing called?
> I forgot . . .

Each of the four Denver schools had some programs to overcome these obstacles (see chapter 4). Yet, despite these resources, many students had only a vague sense of what they would actually do in college, what it takes to succeed there, and how a college education might lead to a job or career:

> RESEARCHER: OK, so we brought this up a little bit earlier, but do you know something that you might major in?
> ALFONSO (Chavez): Like, cars, I have always wanted to know how to fix them and design them and everything. I like to, like, draw. Sometimes I like to draw and design cars and everything.

> • • •

> RESEARCHER: Right, well, all the schools you brought up [Colorado School of Mines, University of Colorado Boulder] were really good schools. Have you ever thought about what you want to major in?
> ANTONY (Chavez): Some kind of engineering, I know that for sure. I think I can make it into it. I have not decided what type of specific engineering; I haven't learned the types of engineering cuz I know that there is a difference and a whole ton of them. And I need to find out which one I like the most and just major in that one.

> • • •

> RESEARCHER: Is there any kind of engineering you're interested in?
> PHILIP (Pella): Probably mechanical engineering.

RESEARCHER: Cool. Have you ever been able to talk to a mechanical engineer or learn much about it?

PHILIP: No, I have not.

. . .

RESEARCHER: Where do you picture yourself after [college]?

SANDER (Southside): Applying for NASA.

RESEARCHER: Doing what?

SANDER: I don't know. I have not thought about that much. I would like to be an astronaut, but there are very low chances, and I do not want to get my hopes up . . . But they [NASA] have a lot of jobs, and I want to work for them.

. . .

RESEARCHER: Can you see yourself going to college to major in . . . sciences or math, since you said you were pretty good in both topics?

PENNY (Pella): I just don't know what opportunities are out there for that. I mean, I know that for science there's chemical engineering 'cause that's the road my brother took, and like, other than that, other than being a math or science teacher, I really do not know any of the jobs that are out there for that.

Students at Capital in Denver were the only ones who routinely articulated specific knowledge of the steps they could take to improve their chances of getting into a "good college." The following excerpts from our interviews make clear the contrast between Capital students and those at the other sampled institutions in Denver and Buffalo:

CATHERINE (Capital): My counselor told me that colleges look for four consecutive years of the same language. You can't switch it up and take four years of four different languages, 'cause then you are just a beginner in everything.

Later, Catherine talked about taking both Geometry and Algebra II in her sophomore year:

RESEARCHER: Why did you decide to take the two together?
CATHERINE: I wanted to take Precalc junior year so I can take AP Calc senior year . . . [And] the teacher recommended me to take two math classes, so I took them. I didn't want to have a bunch of homework, but then, I was like oooooh, I want a 5.0 GPA, so I will take Honors because colleges look at your unweighted GPA.

• • •

RESEARCHER AT CAPITAL: What do you think colleges look for in an applicant?
CHARLES: Test scores . . . ACT and SAT, you gotta do well on them, . . . and I've heard [you need] a lot of good recommendations from teachers. If you have a teacher that sees that you're passionate about something, even though you're not the best student in the class, and they're able to get that on paper, I've heard that can take you way past other applicants. If you have a teacher that knows you well enough to say they're not my best student, but I can see when I'm teaching them that they're here because they want to be, that is beyond helpful.

This kind of talk about what to do to improve one's chances of getting into a "good college" was not heard at Chavez, Pella, or Southside in Denver.

Although it might be argued that nationally the vast majority of students do not have a firm understanding of these particulars prior to attending postsecondary institutions, it can also be argued that students in more privileged schools are able to draw on the knowledge and experiences of parents, guardians, older siblings, and close community members who attended college and have good careers. This information is also routinely communicated to students in public and private high schools that serve more economically privileged populations, beginning as early as grade 9 and intensifying in grades 11 and 12. These schools make it their business to communicate to students and parents a range of information linked to preparation for college, including test-taking options (ACT versus SAT), constructing college entrance essays, scaffolding for acceptance at particularly located colleges, and specific requirements for potential entrance to majors like engineering.[20] While the Buffalo schools could potentially compensate for this lack of knowledge through sustained programming that delivers it directly, this is not, by and large, the case, even in schools such as STEM Academy and Global Horizons that opened under the auspices of College Board. As discussed in chapter 4, the Denver study schools offered various college-linking programs that did a better job providing some information about college preparation for students whose families and communities did not routinely have it.

The Influence of Popular Culture in Buffalo

In the absence of authentic knowledge about college preparation and college-linking processes, some students in Buffalo drew on information embedded in popular culture to inform themselves about college and STEM careers:

> RESEARCHER: Now when you graduate from high school, what do you think you want to do? Do you have any ideas?
>
> FRANCIS (Global Horizons): Yes. I want to go to Stanford, and after that, I want to be a lawyer.
>
> RESEARCHER: Why Stanford?
>
> FRANCIS: I don't know, there's just something about it, I've always wanted to go.
>
> RESEARCHER: Do you remember how you heard about it or how you knew about it?
>
> FRANCIS: [I heard it] on *Hannah Montana*.[21] It's so, I've never told anyone that.

When later asked whether she knew much about Stanford, the following exchange ensued:

RESEARCHER: And knowing what schools are looking for, have you started preparing yourself?

FRANCIS: Yes, I have been trying, like, looking on the website for Stanford, but I really haven't found any information.

Later, in a separate interview, Dannika indicated that she would like to be lawyer or a physician.

RESEARCHER: Why do you want to be a lawyer?

DANNIKA (Global Horizons): I was watching, because I was watching *Law and Order*, and it looks, as yeah, I'm really into it, yeah, lawyers and stuff. I just don't want to be a criminal lawyer.

RESEARCHER: What makes you want to be a doctor?

DANNIKA: I like the show *Grey's Anatomy*. That show, it's a doctor show. It's like, that show makes me so happy. I want to feel someone's heart. I know it sounds creepy, but I really want to put my hands inside someone, working on them.

Similarly at STEM Academy, Dion hoped to be a lawyer and was also influenced by images produced by popular culture.

DION: I want to go to a college that has Pre-law. I want to be a lawyer.

RESEARCHER: Pre-law. How did you get into that?

DION: I don't know. I just like watching the TV shows, like *Law and Order*.

RESEARCHER: Any others?

DION: I just like law. I want to learn it.

Although these students were imagining futures in specific high-level career areas, often linked to a STEM field, they were configuring their understandings based on television images. Television images found their way into the largely blank space of authentic information about college and potential careers, as students developed their own understanding about schools and potential careers, leaving them to construct images of science, math, and law from television shows that simplify, romanticize, and distort these fields with no clear understanding of what it takes to pursue them.

OPPORTUNITY STRUCTURES, FIGURED WORLDS, AND IDENTITIES

High school opportunity structures and figured worlds establish the framework for students' identity development in high school math and science. In neither Denver nor Buffalo were opportunity structures for math and science in our study schools what they might have been; nor were they what was promised when the recent STEM school reform efforts began in the two cities. In neither Denver nor Buffalo did the figured worlds of being good in math or science support the development of authentic, in-depth knowledge in these subject areas. But the limitations in Buffalo were more serious than those in Denver. In Denver, the focal students had access to advanced math and science courses, took these courses, and proceeded through them in a coherent sequence. This was not the case in Buffalo. In Denver, the figured world of being good in math or science focused primarily on procedural details and behavioral compliance but also conveyed desirable high-status identities and the promise of college and career success on those who succeeded in terms of the figured world that circulated at their schools. This was not the case in Buffalo. There, high school opportunity structures did not offer consistent, coherent, or well-sequenced advanced math and science courses. Rather, "shadow capital" characterized the math and science knowledge presented to students. Further, course and programmatic "bait and switch" maneuvers, such as those we saw at Broadway Science in chapter 3, left students with little to no dominant STEM capital to exchange for placement or success in college STEM; and college and career counselors were regularly diverted to other tasks, including that of "graduation cop." In this situation, the likelihood is much lower than among our Denver sample that students will develop or sustain identities with authentic interests in math or science, will come to perform "well" by dominant standards in these fields, will want or be able to pursue math or science in college or beyond, or will be successful if they choose to try. Even those students designated as "high achieving" in this context will likely be ill-prepared and uninclined to pursue higher education in math or science.

• • •

In the next chapter, we examine the postsecondary and career outcomes of the focal students in Denver and Buffalo. These findings suggest the accumulated consequences of the opportunity structures and figured worlds we found in the two cities.

CHAPTER 6

Educational and Occupational Outcomes

I n the preceding chapters, we showed how the various mechanisms of erosion, diversion, and hollowing out undermined initial hopes and plans to increase STEM opportunities for historically minoritized students. We also showed that although these mechanisms were in place in the schools we studied in both cities, their effects were more virulent in Buffalo than in Denver, and erosion of STEM programs and course offerings was more pronounced. The diversion of in-school counseling away from high-achieving students was nearly total in both cities, but in Denver (unlike in Buffalo), college and career counseling continued to be offered through external partnerships with local colleges and nonprofit organizations. The figured worlds of "being good" in school math or science were hollowed out in both cities, but in different ways and with implications that provided more short- and long-term potential for students in Denver.

The multiyear follow-up data we highlight in this chapter suggest that the short- and likely long-term consequences of these differences were quite profound. Although the focal students in our study were initially well matched—both demographically (especially if Capital is omitted) and academically (top 20 percent of their class relative to their school based on ninth-grade standardized test scores)—the students' college and career trajectories with regard to STEM diverged quite dramatically in undergraduate and graduate education as well as in subsequent employment.

This situation is reminiscent of examples used by scholars who have focused on how social advantages and disadvantages accumulate over time to (re)produce inequality.[1] Their theories of "cumulative advantage" or "cumulative disadvantage" posit that events leading to advantage or disadvantage accumulate such that initially similar people or groups *become* dissimilar over time as "hardships in multiple domains pile up for certain individuals and not others."[2] In our case, it appears that fairly small advantages related to STEM opportunities accumulated for the Denver students as relative disadvantages accumulated for those in Buffalo, leading to significant differences in postsecondary outcomes.[3]

FOLLOW-UP STUDY, 2015–2019: OVERVIEW OF OUTCOMES

Outcome data were gathered as follows: (1) an online descriptive survey administered to all focal students whom we were able to locate in 2015, two years after graduation from high school; and (2) face-to-face or remote Zoom/FaceTime/Skype interviews with as many of the original focal students as possible from each city, from 2017 through 2019.[4] Data sources for this chapter additionally include: (1) published ninth- through twelfth-grade course offerings; and (2) official student transcripts gathered for all focal students at the end of each cohort's senior year of high school. Individual student transcripts provided data on actual math and science courses taken over the course of the students' four years in high school. Of particular interest are math and science course-taking patterns for AP and IB courses within and across each city.

Follow-up data enabled us to assess actual enrollment in college as well as the extent to which students pursued a STEM major, graduated from a four- or two-year institution, graduated in STEM, pursued a further degree in STEM, or took up a STEM career (see the appendix for additional details). This analysis includes those who said they intended to pursue a college STEM major during their final year in high school, as well as those who did not express such intent. In considering the data in this chapter, it is important to note that although focal students at Denver's Capital High were racially and ethnically diverse, they by and large came from somewhat more highly economically capitalized families than students at the other sampled schools (see chapter 1).

Of the original forty-eight Denver focal students, we reinterviewed or have survey data from thirty-seven of them. To be clear, we could not locate or interview every student in either city at the two points in time (2015 and 2017 through 2019). Only those students for whom we have a complete set of information with respect to: (1) college attendance (four or two year, or none); (2) graduation from a four- or two-year institution (yes or no); and (3) college major (STEM or not STEM) were included for purposes of analysis in this chapter. In Denver, thirty-seven of the original forty-eight focal students were the n for this group. We collected the same data from the Buffalo students, where again, despite our best efforts, we were not able to reconnect with all focal students at the two points in time. Of the original forty-eight focal students in Buffalo, we have complete follow-up information for twenty-six of them. This comprised the n for the Buffalo group discussed in this chapter. It was more difficult to reconnect with students from Buffalo than Denver (see the appendix). It was easiest to reconnect with the somewhat more highly capitalized Capital students in Denver, as well as gather supplemental data about them from internet searches, because they had the strongest digital footprint among the group.

At the end of grade 9 (2009), when we first met the students, a key metric for focal student selection was expressed interest in pursuing STEM in college and career (see chapter 1 and the appendix). By their senior year of high school, twenty-five of the thirty-seven (68 percent) original Denver focal students from whom we were able to collect follow-up data had informed us that they intended to pursue some type of STEM major in college. The remaining students either were not sure of their intended major or intended to pursue majors that were not STEM related.

Table 6.1 summarizes the follow-up data for the thirty-seven Denver participants for whom we were able to obtain complete data. Among them, 65 percent attended a four-year college or university; 19 percent attended a two-year college; and 16 percent did not attend any postsecondary institution. Overall, Denver college graduation outcomes for the thirty-seven participants were as follows: 62 percent graduated from a four-year school; 8 percent graduated from a two-year school; and

TABLE 6.1 *Postsecondary outcomes, Denver**

SCHOOL NAME	TOTAL # OF PARTICIPANTS	ATTENDED 4-YEAR COLLEGE	ATTENDED 2-YEAR COLLEGE	DID NOT ATTEND COLLEGE	GRADUATED FROM 4-YEAR COLLEGE	GRADUATED FROM 2-YEAR COLLEGE	DID NOT GRADUATE FROM COLLEGE
Chavez	9	44% (n = 4)	33% (n = 3)	22% (n = 2)	44% (n = 4)	22% (n = 2)	33% (n = 3)
Pella**	10	70% (n = 7)	0% (n = 0)	30% (n = 3)	60% (n = 6)	0% (n = 0)	40% (n = 4)
Southside	7	29% (n = 2)	57% (n = 4)	14% (n = 1)	29% (n = 2)	14% (n = 1)	57% (n = 4)
Capital	11	100% (n = 11)	0% (n = 0)	0% (n = 0)	100% (n = 11)	0% (n = 0)	0% (n = 0)
All 4 Denver schools	37	65% (n = 24)	19% (n = 7)	16% (n = 6)	62% (n = 23)	8% (n = 3)	30% (n = 11)
Denver schools (minus Capital)	26	50% (n = 13)	27% (n = 7)	23% (n = 6)	46% (n = 12)	12% (n = 3)	42% (n = 11)

*Percentages in this table have been rounded and may not total to 100%.

**Two Pella participants (20% of the Pella sample) entered the military after high school in lieu of college. One participant, Paula, entered the military, became chronically ill, and did not pursue further education or employment. The other participant, Pacco, entered the military, was trained in aviation electronics technology, became an aviation electronics technician in the military, and is still serving in that capacity.

30 percent did not graduate from a four- or two-year postsecondary institution. Removing Capital from the analysis, we found the following: 50 percent attended a four-year college, 27 percent attended a two-year college, and 23 percent did not attend college. Without Capital, 46 percent graduated from a four-year institution, 12 percent graduated from a two-year institution, and 42 percent did not graduate from a four- or two-year postsecondary institution.

For Buffalo, table 6.2 summarizes the follow-up data from twenty-six students. Among them, 58 percent attended a four-year college, 38 percent attended a two-year school, and 4 percent did not attend college. Here, if Capital is excluded, a considerably higher percentage of Buffalo follow-up students attended some college after graduating from high school than in Denver, with more Buffalo students choosing two-year colleges. Turning to college graduation rates in Buffalo, 42 percent graduated from a four-year college, 19 percent from a two-year college, and 38 percent did not graduate from a four- or a two-year college. If Capital is excluded, overall college graduation rates are more closely aligned across the schools in the two cities. Statistical test results also support the point that graduation rates by sector of postsecondary institution were not significantly different between Buffalo and Denver: when Capital students are excluded, $(2, N = 52) = 0.59, p > .05$.

Table 6.3 reports percent postsecondary STEM graduation rates by city and school for all focal students for whom we have follow-up data. Fifty-one percent of the original thirty-seven Denver focal students completed some form of STEM major in college, either four or two year. When we remove Capital from the calculation, 38 percent of the remaining Denver students graduated with a STEM major from college.

As tables 6.3 and 6.4 collectively show, 50 percent ($n = 3$ of 6) of students from STEM Academy, an inclusive STEM high school in Buffalo, graduated with a postsecondary STEM major, with two students among this group (two of three, 67 percent) graduating from a four-year school and one student (one of three, 33 percent) graduating from a two-year school. *Not a single student from Broadway Science, our second Buffalo inclusive STEM school, graduated with a STEM major from either a four- or two-year institution.* In the two STEM-focused schools in Denver, Chavez

TABLE 6.2 *Postsecondary outcomes, Buffalo**

SCHOOL NAME	TOTAL # OF PARTICIPANTS	ATTENDED 4-YEAR COLLEGE	ATTENDED 2-YEAR COLLEGE	DID NOT ATTEND COLLEGE	GRADUATED FROM 4-YEAR COLLEGE	GRADUATED FROM 2-YEAR COLLEGE	DID NOT GRADUATE FROM COLLEGE
Broadway Science Academy	5	60% (n = 3)	40% (n = 2)	0% (n = 0)	20% (n = 1)	0% (n = 0)	80% (n = 4)
STEM Academy	6	83% (n = 5)	17% (n = 1)	0% (n = 0)	67% (n = 4)	17% (n = 1)	17% (n = 1)
Global Horizons	11	27% (n = 3)	64% (n = 7)	9% (n = 1)	27% (n = 3)	36% (n = 4)	36% (n = 4)
Lincoln	4	100% (n = 4)	0% (n = 0)	0% (n = 0)	75% (n = 3)	0% (n = 0)	25% (n = 1)
All 4 Buffalo schools	26	58% (n = 15)	38% (n = 10)	4% (n = 1)	42% (n = 11)	19% (n = 5)	38% (n = 10)

*Percentages in this table have been rounded and may not total to 100%.

TABLE 6.3 *STEM degree completion by school, Denver and Buffalo**

HIGH SCHOOL ATTENDED	TOTAL # OF PARTICIPANTS	COMPLETED STEM MAJOR IN POSTSECONDARY INSTITUTION
Denver		
Chavez	9	44% (*n* = 4)
Pella	10	40% (*n* = 4)
Southside	7	29% (*n* = 2)
Capital	11	82% (*n* = 9)
Total (all 4 schools)	37	51% (*n* = 19)
Total (minus Capital)	26	38% (*n* = 10)
Buffalo		
Broadway Science Academy	5	0% (*n* = 0)
STEM Academy	6	50% (*n* = 3)
Global Horizons	11	36% (*n* = 4)
Lincoln	4	25% (*n* = 1)
Total	26	31% (*n* = 8)

*Percentages in this table have been rounded and may not total to 100%.

TABLE 6.4 *Proportion of 4-year and 2-year STEM degree completion among those who finished a postsecondary STEM degree, Denver and Buffalo**

HIGH SCHOOL ATTENDED	PROPORTION OF STEM MAJORS COMPLETED AT 4-YEAR POSTSECONDARY INSTITUTION	PROPORTION OF STEM MAJORS COMPLETED AT 2-YEAR POSTSECONDARY INSTITUTION
Denver (*n* = 19)		
Chavez	75% (*n* = 3)	25% (*n* = 1)
Pella	100% (*n* = 4)	0% (*n* = 0)
Southside	50% (*n* = 1)	50% (*n* = 1)
Capital	100% (*n* = 9)	0% (*n* = 0)
Total (all 4 schools)	89%	11%
Total (minus Capital)	80%	20%
Buffalo (*n* = 8)		
Broadway Science Academy	0% (*n* = 0)	0% (*n* = 0)
STEM Academy	67% (*n* = 2)	33% (*n* = 1)
Global Horizons	25% (*n* = 1)	75% (*n* = 3)
Lincoln	100% (*n* = 1)	0% (*n* = 0)
Total	50%	50%

*Percentages in this table have been rounded and may not total to 100%.

and Pella, we found the following: Forty-four percent of students from Chavez (four of nine) graduated with a STEM degree. Among those Chavez students who graduated in STEM, 75 percent (three of four) graduated with a four-year degree and 25 percent (one of four) graduated with a two-year degree. At Pella, 40 percent of students (four of ten) graduated in STEM. Among these STEM graduates, 100 percent graduated from a four-year institution.

Among the focal students from Buffalo's Global Horizons (a comprehensive school) with whom we followed up, 36 percent (four of eleven) graduated with a STEM degree, with 25 percent (one of four) graduating from a four-year institution and 75 percent (three of four) graduating from a two-year institution. In contrast, at Southside, our second comprehensive school in Denver, 29 percent (two of seven) graduated with a STEM degree, with one student graduating from a four-year institution and one from a two-year institution. All of the focal students at Capital, a Denver comprehensive school, graduated from a four-year institution, with nine of the eleven (82 percent) graduating with a STEM major.

Given the figures in tables 6.1, 6.2, 6.3 and 6.4, the following points are particularly noteworthy: When we remove Capital students from Denver analyses and compare STEM degree completion across the two cities (not taking into account four-year versus two-year graduation rates in STEM), we find reasonable comparability with respect to earning STEM degrees, with 38 percent obtaining STEM degrees in Denver and 31 percent in Buffalo. Statistical test results also indicate that the percentage of students who earned a STEM degree did not significantly differ across the two cities, when we remove Capital students: $(1, N = 52) = 0.34$, $p > .05$. However, not a single student from Broadway Science—one of two sampled STEM schools in Buffalo—majored in STEM and obtained a STEM degree at *any* postsecondary institution, four or two year. Only one student from Broadway Science earned a college degree, in this case, from a four-year institution.

In striking contrast to Broadway Science, at our two sampled STEM focused schools in Denver, 44 percent of students from Chavez earned a STEM degree and 40 percent from Pella earned a STEM degree. Among these students, 88 percent (seven of eight) of the students from Chavez and Pella collectively earned a STEM degree from a four-year institution. This compares with 67 percent (two of three) at Buffalo's STEM Academy who earned a STEM degree at a four-year institution and 0 percent at Buffalo's Broadway Science who earned a STEM degree at *either* a four- or two-year school. Importantly, in Denver, minus Capital, 80 percent (eight of ten) of those earning STEM degrees earned them in a four-year institution. In Buffalo, 50 percent of all students who earned STEM degrees earned them in a four-year college. Having said this, as numbers in each category are small, we must be very cautious about interpretation.

HIGH SCHOOL STEM COURSE-TAKING, INTENDED MAJOR IN HIGH SCHOOL, COLLEGE MAJOR, AND CURRENT OCCUPATION: DENVER AND BUFFALO

High School STEM Course-Taking

As we point out in chapter 2, during the period immediately preceding and including our on-site ethnographic investigation, the total number of math and science courses officially offered at three of the four Denver schools increased, as did the number of advanced courses, including honors (considered more advanced than regular courses, but not as rigorous as AP or IB; see table 2.3 in chapter 2). Although course data were not exactly comparable in the two cities, the robust increases seen in Denver did not occur in Buffalo, which also had few differences between STEM-focused and comprehensive schools. Smaller in size than the Denver schools, the Buffalo schools had more limited higher-level math and science course offerings in the form of AP and Regents courses. The AP courses declined at both the STEM-focused and comprehensive schools in Buffalo during the period of our investigation (see table 2.4 in chapter 2 for detailed information on non-Regents, Regents, and AP math and science course offerings in Buffalo during the period of our study).

In 2010, Buffalo's Broadway Science offered six Regents courses in math and science—Biology, Earth Science, Algebra I, Geometry, Algebra II/ Trigonometry, and Precalculus—but offered *no* AP courses. This means that in 2010, when our site-based study was just beginning, students in a designated STEM school—in this case, Broadway Science—had *no* access to courses in math or science above the Regents level, in spite of district promises to the contrary when the school opened as a STEM school. While relatively challenging compared to non-Regents courses in New York State and necessary for graduation from high school, New York Regents courses do not compare with the demanding nature of AP or IB courses, and one only needs to score a 65 on the Regents examination to pass the course for purposes of high school graduation. As we note in chapter 3, Regents offerings in STEM also eroded over the course of our three-year ethnographic study.

In this chapter, we focus specifically on *advanced math and science course-taking, as recorded on the official transcripts of our follow-up focal students*, in order to examine the relationship between *actual* advanced math and science course-taking in high school, postsecondary entrance and graduation patterns, and completion of a college STEM major. While quantitative research has explored these relationships, noting the importance of high-level mathematics courses in particular, no study, to date, has tracked ethnographically how the system created by opportunity structures manifests in the high school to college trajectories of individual students over time.[5] This is particularly critical in light of expressed intent to broaden opportunities for low-income and minoritized students via intensification of high school STEM curricular offerings and programming.

High school transcripts document all math and science courses taken by individual focal students in the eight sampled schools in Denver and Buffalo, from first year of high school (grade 9) through fourth year (grade 12). Consistent with prior analyses in this chapter, the student sample includes only those individuals who participated in our follow-up study. Also here, we define advanced courses *solely* as AP and IB, eliminating honors and Regents courses from the analysis.[6] Given challenges associated with finding students post-high school and, in some cases, having students agree to follow-up interviews or surveys, our follow-up sample (total two-city sample, $n = 63$: Buffalo, $n = 26$; Denver, $n = 37$) represents, in all likelihood, those students who were most successful post-high school, as they would be most likely to agree to speak with us. We therefore suspect that the available data *overesti-mate* the degree to which the full complement of ninety-six original focal students achieved goals aligned with the STEM reform effort.

Table 6.5 shows advanced (AP or IB) course-taking among the thirty-seven Denver students for whom we have complete follow-up data. Forty-nine percent (eighteen of thirty-seven) of the Denver portion of the follow-up group took advanced STEM courses as defined in this chapter. Data are reported by student race/ethnicity, gender, and high school attended. Among those reinterviewed, *all* eleven Capital students completed advanced high school STEM courses, with all students subsequently attending and graduating from a public or private four-year postsecondary institution. In contrast, only one of the nine reinterviewed Denver Chavez students took advanced high school STEM courses. Four of the ten Pella students took advanced STEM coursework in high school, while two of the Southside students completed AP or IB STEM courses. Although not shown in table 6.5, the Denver students who took advanced math or science progressed through established sequences of high school math and science courses—for example, from Algebra II/Trig to Precalculus to Calculus and from (regular) Biology to Chemistry to Physics or AP Biology.

Across the four institutions in Denver, students in the follow-up group took an average of 2.4 advanced STEM courses. Eighteen of these courses were taken by the eleven follow-up students from Capital, while the remaining twenty-six courses were taken by seven students at the other three schools, for a total of forty-four advanced STEM courses taken by eighteen students. At Capital, the average number of advanced STEM courses per student was 1.6, and we see that every single student in the follow-up group at Capital took at least one advanced course. In contrast, only 27 percent (seven of the remaining twenty-six) of students in our follow-up study at Chavez, Pella, and Southside took advanced courses. What we see here, then, is that Capital students in the follow-up group were much more likely to have completed AP courses, while only a small number of reinterviewed focal students at the other three Denver schools completed advanced STEM courses as defined in this chapter.

TABLE 6.5 *AP/IB STEM course-taking in high school (follow-up focal students only), Denver*

(n = 18)

Name of student	Grade 9 math	Grade 10 math	Grade 11 math	Grade 12 math	Grade 9 science	Grade 10 science	Grade 11 science	Grade 12 science
Chavez (n = 1)								
Anne (White, Female)			IB Math 1	IB Math 2		IB Chemistry	IB Biology 1	IB Biology 1
Pella (n = 4)								
Padma (Asian, Female)			IB Math 1	IB Math 2			IB Biology 1; IB Environmental Systems	AP Chemistry; IB Biology 2
Pahal (Asian, Female)			IB Math 1	IB Math 2			IB Biology 1	IB Biology 2
Prak (Asian, Male)			IB Math 1	IB Math 2			IB Biology 1	IB Biology 2
Paula (White, Female)							IB Physics	
Southside (n = 2)								
Selena (Latina, Female)				AP Calculus AB			AP Physics	AP Biology
Sofia (Latina, Female)				AP Calculus AB			AP Physics	AP Biology
Capital (n = 11)								
Candalaria (Latina, Female)				AP Calculus AB				AP Biology

Note: AP = Advanced Placement; IB = International Baccalaureate; AB = Highest level of course; BC = Second-highest level of course.

TABLE 6.5 *Continued*

($n = 18$)

Name of student	Grade 9 math	Grade 10 math	Grade 11 math	Grade 12 math	Grade 9 science	Grade 10 science	Grade 11 science	Grade 12 science
Capital ($n = 11$)								
César (Latino, Male)				AP Calculus BC			AP Chemistry	AP Biology
Chang (Asian, Female)				AP Calculus AB				
Catherine (Black, Female)				AP Calculus AB				AP Biology
Carlos (Latino, Male)				AP Calculus AB				AP Biology
Chaquille (Black, Male)			AP Calculus AB				AP Chemistry	AP Biology
Chandra (Black, Female)				AP Calculus AB				AP Biology
Cailey (Black, Female)								AP Biology
Carolynne (Black, Female)				AP Calculus AB				AP Biology
Charles (White, Male)								AP Biology
Candace (Asian, Female)							AP Environmental Science	

Note: AP = Advanced Placement; IB = International Baccalaureate; AB = Highest level of course; BC = Second-highest level of course.

Table 6.6 lists the advanced STEM courses (AP and IB) taken by Buffalo focal students in the follow-up group. Unlike in Denver, where we see forty-four advanced STEM courses taken by eighteen Denver students, only six Buffalo students, all at one school, took even a *single* advanced STEM course. When we compare the number of advanced STEM courses taken by the follow-up students, minus Capital, there were twenty-six courses in Denver and ten in Buffalo. In other words, there were more than double the number of advanced courses taken by about the same number of students in the Denver sample at three of the four Denver schools (Chavez, Pella, and Southside, $n = 26$ students, 26 courses) as there were in the four-school Buffalo sample ($n = 26$ students, 10 courses). Further, when comparing only advanced mathematics coursework across the two cities, it appeared that Denver students were more likely to take advanced mathematics courses than Buffalo students ($(1, n = 63) = 12.65, p < .001$).

Clearly, the quick elimination of advanced STEM courses in Buffalo, as pointed out in chapter 3, accounts for the relatively low number of students who took them, as advanced STEM courses were simply no longer offered. This point does not pertain to AP courses only; in fact, by the second year of our study, some of our sampled Buffalo schools offered a very small number of *any higher-level core STEM courses*, whether AP, honors, Regents, *or* regular. For example, the highest-level math course offered at Broadway Science was Regents Algebra II/Trigonometry. There was no Precalculus or Calculus offered at any level—non-Regents, Regents, or AP. The highest-level science courses that Broadway Science offered were Regents Earth Science, which is normally offered in eighth or ninth grade in New York State, and Regents Biology (normally a tenth-grade course)—with one section of regular Chemistry. There were non-Regents/regular courses offered in subjects like Forensics and Anatomy & Physiology. Lincoln offered no Regents science course beyond Chemistry, which was, in fact, canceled, without prior notice, at the very beginning of the final year of our in-school study. This means that Lincoln offered no Physics course at any level, and, by the final year of our study, no Chemistry course at any level either. Global Horizons offered Regents Algebra II/Trigonometry as its highest-level math course,

TABLE 6.6 *AP/IB STEM course-taking in high school (follow-up focal students only), Buffalo*

Name of student	Grade 9 math	Grade 10 math	Grade 11 math	Grade 12 math	Grade 9 science	Grade 10 science	Grade 11 science	Grade 12 science
STEM Academy ($n = 6$)								
Paul (White, Male)							AP Environmental Science	
Jada (Black, Female)						AP Biology	AP Environmental Science	
Dillon (Black, Male)						AP Biology	AP Environmental Science	
Jayme (Black, Female)								AP Environmental Science
Robert (White, Male)						AP Biology	AP Environmental Science	
Isaac (Black, Male)						AP Biology	AP Environmental Science	

Note: AP = Advanced Placement

with Regents Biology and Regents Chemistry offered as its highest-level Regents science courses.

The only school among sampled Buffalo institutions to offer Physics was Global Horizons, and this was offered at the regular level. STEM Academy was the only school to offer *any* AP STEM courses—in this case, AP Chemistry, AP Environmental Science, and AP Anatomy & Physiology. STEM Academy was also the only school to offer Calculus among the sampled Buffalo schools, but only at the regular level. In point of fact, despite promises to the contrary, within a very short period of time *all higher-level core math/science STEM courses*—whether at the AP, Regents, *or* regular (non-Regents) level—were simply expunged from the sampled Buffalo schools' lists of active offerings. Such courses are presumably standard fare among high school offerings in math and science in US high schools. As we see here, however, initially offered higher-level STEM courses were not sustained, including in the two newly opened STEM schools.

According to the Office of Civil Rights Data Collection on STEM Course Taking, advanced mathematics was offered at 65 percent of US high schools in 2015–16, and Calculus was offered at 50 percent of high schools in the same period. For schools with high Black and Latino/a student enrollment, however, advanced mathematics courses were offered at only 55 percent of schools and Calculus was offered at 38 percent of schools.[7] The lack of advanced STEM courses is especially noteworthy, of course, at schools that marketed themselves as newly launched and upgraded STEM schools aimed at providing broadened opportunities for high-level STEM in college and career for low-income and minoritized students. As we see here, the lack of advanced STEM courses was more characteristic of the sampled institutions in Buffalo than in Denver. A few advanced-level STEM courses were eliminated in Denver as well, but some advanced courses remained in both math and science at all four Denver schools. The falloff that occurred in Denver was the elimination of the IB diploma programs at Chavez and Pella, but the IB STEM courses themselves remained for the duration of our study.

Although the meaningful high-level vision for STEM began to unravel in the sampled Buffalo schools during the first year of our study and was, for all practical purposes, obsolete by the third year, Buffalo focal students remained interested in the promise of STEM—42 percent still planned to declare a STEM major in college during their senior year of high school. As will become clearer in this chapter, however, the exchange value of the STEM courses that Buffalo students were able to take and complete was relatively low in comparison to the exchange value of math and science courses available to and taken by the Denver focal students over the course of high school. For Buffalo students who had initially expressed and then retained interest in pursuing STEM in college, inequalities continued to deepen in relation to the Denver sample moving forward, reflective of a highly unequal capital accumulation process linked, in this case, specifically to STEM.[8]

As we note at the beginning of this chapter, theories of "cumulative advantage" or "disadvantage" suggest that events leading to relative advantage or disadvantage *accumulate*, such that initially similar people or groups *become* increasingly dissimilar over time. As we will see even more clearly in the next section of this chapter, relatively small advantages with respect to STEM opportunities "piled up" in multiple domains, such as availability of advanced math and science courses and counseling for college and STEM in Denver, whereas relatively small disadvantages "piled up" in these same multiple domains in Buffalo, leading to notable differences in postsecondary outcomes.

College Type, Competitiveness, STEM Degrees, and STEM Employment

Tables 6.7 and 6.8 examine college type, proximity from home, institutional selectivity (a measure of competitiveness), and whether or not students graduated from these institutions. These tables report data by city and school for all sampled students for whom we have follow-up data and who graduated *in STEM* from a postsecondary institution.

Looking carefully at the undergraduate institutions attended by the follow-up students who graduated in STEM is particularly revealing with respect to the issues at hand. When we analyze STEM college graduation data from the Denver follow-up group, including Capital, 74 percent (fourteen of nineteen) of Denver students who graduated in STEM

TABLE 6.7 *Name, college type, proximity, selectivity, and graduation status of students who majored in STEM, Denver*

NAME	COLLEGE TYPE (4 YEAR OR 2 YEAR)	COLLEGE PROXIMITY FROM HOME (MILES)	SELECTIVITY CATEGORY INDEX*	GRADUATED? Y/N
		(n = 19)		
Chavez (n = 4)				
Alice	4	< 10	VC	Y
Ana	4	< 120	C	Y
Adriana	4	< 10	VC	Y
Anne	2	< 10	NR	Y
Pella (n = 4)				
Padma	4	< 120	VC+	Y
Penny	4	< 10	NR	Y
Pahal	4	< 120	VC	Y
Prak	4	< 10	VC	Y
Southside (n = 2)				
Selena	4	< 10	HC	Y
Sokhem	2	< 10	NR	Y
Capital (n = 9)				
Candalaria	4	< 120	HC+	Y
César	4	> 1,000	HC+	Y
Chang	4	< 120	VC	Y
Catherine	4	< 1,000	VC	Y
Carlos	4	< 10	VC	Y
Chaquille	4	> 1,000	MC	Y
Chandra	4	> 1,000	VC	Y
Cailey	4	< 120	C	Y
Carolynne	4	< 10	VC+	Y

*Selectivity category index adapted from Barron's 2013 Index of College Selectivity (MC = Most Competitive; HC+ = Highly Competitive+; HC = Highly Competitive; VC+ = Very Competitive+; VC = Very Competitive; C = Competitive; NR = Not Ranked [4-year colleges not ranked in Barron's 2013 Profiles of American Colleges, including all 2-year institutions]). For our purposes in this chapter, the "top" category includes MC, HC+, HC, VC+, and VC schools.

did so from either well-known four-year private institutions, flagship state institutions, or smaller four-year institutions ranked Most Competitive (MC), Highly Competitive+ (HC+), Highly Competitive (HC), Very Competitive+ (VC+), or Very Competitive (VC)—our "top" category.[9] When we remove Capital from the analysis, 60 percent (six of ten) of the

TABLE 6.8 *Name, college type, proximity, selectivity, and graduation status of students who majored in STEM, Buffalo*

		(n = 8)		
NAME	COLLEGE TYPE (4-YEAR OR 2-YEAR)	COLLEGE PROXIMITY FROM HOME (MILES)	SELECTIVITY CATEGORY INDEX*	GRADUATED? Y/N
Broadway Science Academy (*n* = 0)				
None				
STEM Academy (*n* = 3)				
Robert	4	< 10	VC	Y
Jayme	2	< 120	NR	Y
Isaac	4	< 1,000	VC	Y
Global Horizons (*n* = 4)				
Sofian	2	< 10	NR	Y
Matthew	4	< 120	C	Y
Mya	2	< 10	NR	Y
Sarah	2	< 10	NR	Y
Lincoln (*n* = 1)				
Sadie	4	< 10	VC+	Y

*Selectivity category index adapted from Barron's 2013 Index of College Selectivity (MC = Most Competitive; HC+ = Highly Competitive+; HC = Highly Competitive; VC+ = Very Competitive+; VC = Very Competitive; C = Competitive; NR = Not Ranked [4-year colleges not ranked in Barron's 2013 Profiles of American Colleges, including all 2-year institutions]). For our purposes in this chapter, the "top" category includes MC, HC+, HC, VC+, and VC schools.

remaining Denver follow-up students who were accepted at, attended (for their first degree), and graduated in STEM did so at institutions of comparable competitiveness levels. By way of example, schools that fell into the MC ranking at the time these participants were entering college (2013) included Princeton University, Stanford University, Oberlin College, and Williams College. Schools that fell into the HC+ ranking in 2013 included American University, Skidmore College, and University of Illinois at Urbana-Champaign. HC schools in 2013 included University of Texas at Dallas, Fordham University, and Marquette University. VC+ schools in 2013 included Indiana University Bloomington, Rochester Institute of Technology, and University of Tennessee at Knoxville. VC schools in 2013 included Illinois College, Colorado Christian College, and University of Wisconsin-La Crosse. To be clear, with the exception of the MC category, where schools are overwhelmingly private, a range of public and private institutions are represented in each classificatory category. As we are preserving student and institutional anonymity, these are not the actual names of the institutions attended by the focal students. However, these largely recognizable "name brand" institutions exemplify those in each competitiveness category.

In contrast to Denver, in Buffalo 38 percent (three of eight) of the follow-up focal students, across all four high schools, were accepted at, attended, and graduated in STEM from our constructed "top" category—those colleges ranked as MC, HC+, HC, VC+, or VC. This compares to *60 percent of non-Capital students* who attended a "top" college and graduated in STEM among the Denver sample. As noted earlier, with the inclusion of Capital, a school that serves a *somewhat* more highly economically capitalized student population than the other three Denver schools, the proportion of students who attended colleges in our "top" category rises to 74 percent. Also importantly, unlike Denver, where a notable number of students attended and graduated from the University of Colorado Boulder, Colorado State University, or a similarly ranked public postsecondary institution, only one Buffalo student who graduated in STEM attended the University at Buffalo, a flagship public research university that is well known for its prestigious STEM programs, and *no* students graduated in STEM from a four-year public comprehensive college. In fact, the institutions from which Denver students graduated in STEM were, overall, more highly ranked and well known in STEM areas than those attended by Buffalo students. In this regard, the exchange value of the STEM college degrees earned by Denver students was likely to be higher than the exchange value accrued by Buffalo students. In other words, the post-high school trajectories of Buffalo students make clear that they continued to lose ground, over time, relative to comparably capitalized Denver students. This is the case whether Capital is included in the analysis or not.

One important question remains: to what extent do undergraduate STEM degrees from differentially ranked institutions serve to position students for future postgraduate education and career options in STEM moving forward? Denver's comparative strength becomes that much more apparent when we consider this question. Although the "Capital effect" explains much of the difference in some outcomes in the two cities, deep differences in post-undergraduate outcomes remain highly visible even when we remove Capital from the analysis.

In tables 6.9 and 6.10, we report high school attended, students' race/ethnicity, whether they intended to major in STEM at the end of high school, and post-undergraduate outcomes for all Denver and Buffalo students in the follow-up group who graduated from four- or two-year institutions in STEM. We additionally include Patricia (from Pella in Denver), who, although not having graduated in STEM, is currently working in a STEM field. These tables enable us to compare outcomes among all sampled schools within Denver, within Buffalo, and between Denver and Buffalo. Outcome data include current employment or post-undergraduate education for all (former) focal students who were working in STEM or are pursuing further degrees in STEM.

These tables highlight the apparent exchange value of accrued capital in the trajectories of individual students, over time, as well as the previously noted "Capital effect." For example, in table 6.9, we see that Candalaria, a Latina from Capital, attended an HC+ college and was a medical assistant at a pediatric practice, simultaneously studying for the MCAT; César, a Latino from Capital, attended an HC+ college, and had recently completed Teach for America and had become a math teacher in Denver; Chang, an Asian American female from Capital, who attended a VC college, was pursuing a speech pathology graduate degree; Catherine, a Black female from Capital, attended a VC college and was pursuing a PhD in toxicology. These Capital students were well on their way into professional jobs or postgraduate training at highly competitive universities.

It is also apparent that the "Capital effect" does not *fully* explain different postsecondary outcomes in the two cities, because comparably capitalized students in Buffalo and Denver—minus Capital—were notably different with respect to a range of outcomes. As impressive as Capital's postsecondary STEM outcomes were for our follow-up group, Denver's success in this arena extended beyond Capital. For example, Selena, a Latina who attended Southside, completed a BS in nursing at an HC college; Prak, an Asian American male student from Pella,

TABLE 6.9 Intended and completed STEM major, race/ethnicity, type of postsecondary institution attended, and current employment/educational pursuit, Denver

(n = 20)

NAME	HIGH SCHOOL	RACE/ ETHNICITY*	INTENDED TO PURSUE STEM AT END OF HIGH SCHOOL? Y/N	ATTENDED 4-YEAR OR 2-YEAR COLLEGE?	MAJORED IN STEM IN COLLEGE? Y/N	COLLEGE SELECTIVITY INDEX***	CURRENT EMPLOYMENT/ EDUCATIONAL PURSUIT
Alice	Chavez	L	Y	4	Y	VC	FedEx Ground and Uber employee
Ana	Chavez	L	Y	4	Y	C	Front desk receptionist at a health spa
Adriana	Chavez	L	Y	4	Y	VC	Nurse
Anne	Chavez	W	Y	2	Y	NR	Paramedic
Padma	Pella	A	Y	4	Y	VC+	Working on master's degree in public health
Penny	Pella	W	Y	4	Y	NR	Completed BS degree in math, secondary education concentration
Pahal	Pella	A	N	4	Y	VC	Details not known
Prak	Pella	A	Y	4	Y	VC	Fellow in health-care administration at Sloan Kettering
Patricia**	Pella	L	N	4	N	VC	Community health worker
Selena	Southside	L	Y	4	Y	HC	Obtained a BA in psychology, then returned for and completed a BS in nursing. Completed certification and worked as a certified nurse assistant while completing second BA.

TABLE 6.9 *Continued*

(*n* = 20)

NAME	HIGH SCHOOL	RACE/ ETHNICITY*	INTENDED TO PURSUE STEM AT END OF HIGH SCHOOL? Y/N	ATTENDED 4-YEAR OR 2-YEAR COLLEGE?	MAJORED IN STEM IN COLLEGE? Y/N	COLLEGE SELECTIVITY INDEX***	CURRENT EMPLOYMENT/ EDUCATIONAL PURSUIT
Sokhem	Southside	A	Y	2	Y	NR	Desktop administrator/IT specialist
Candalaria	Capital	L	Y	4	Y	HC+	Medical assistant at pediatric practice while studying for MCAT
César	Capital	L	Y	4	Y	HC+	Completed Teach for America; math teacher in Denver
Chang	Capital	A	Y	4	Y	VC	Speech pathologist graduate student
Catherine	Capital	B	Y	4	Y	VC	PhD student in toxicology
Carlos	Capital	L	Y	4	Y	VC	College admissions counselor
Chaquille	Capital	B	Y	4	Y	MC	Software engineer
Chandra	Capital	B	Y	4	Y	VC	MBA student
Cailey	Capital	B	Y	4	Y	C	Assistant manager at a furniture company
Carolynne	Capital	B	Y	4	Y	VC+	Returned for an accelerated BS in nursing

*In this column, L indicates Latino/a, B indicates Black, W indicates White, and A indicates Asian American.

**Note that Patricia was not a STEM major, but she took a position in the STEM field, as a community health worker, upon graduation from college.

*** Selectivity category index adapted from Barron's 2013 Index of College Selectivity, where MC = Most Competitive; HC+ = Highly Competitive+; HC = Highly Competitive; VC+ = Very Competitive+; VC = Very Competitive; C = Competitive; NR = Not Ranked (4-year colleges not ranked in Barron's 2013 Profiles of American Colleges, including all 2-year institutions). For the purposes of this study, the "top" category includes MC, HC+, HC, VC+, and VC schools.

TABLE 6.10 *Intended and completed STEM major, race/ethnicity, type of postsecondary institution attended, selectivity, and current employment/educational pursuit, Buffalo*

(n = 8)

NAME	HIGH SCHOOL	RACE/ETHNICITY*	INTENDED TO PURSUE STEM AT END OF HIGH SCHOOL? Y/N	ATTENDED 4-YEAR OR 2-YEAR COLLEGE?	MAJORED IN STEM IN COLLEGE? Y/N	SELECTIVITY CATEGORY INDEX**	CURRENT EMPLOYMENT/ EDUCATIONAL STATUS
Robert	STEM Academy	W	Y	4	Y	VC	Roofer
Jayme	STEM Academy	B	N	2	Y	NR	Entered the military after high school, then went on to a 2-year school and completed a degree in digital media. Upon graduation, entered a 4-year program in digital media communications and is currently enrolled in that program
Isaac	STEM Academy	B	N	4	Y	VC	K–12 mathematics teacher
Sofian	Global Horizons	B	N	2	Y	NR	Radiology technician
Matthew	Global Horizons	W	Y	4	Y	C	Owns and manages a construction business
Mya	Global Horizons	A	Y	2	Y	NR	Nurse
Sarah	Global Horizons	A	Y	2	Y	NR	Medical assistant, then practicing nurse
Sadie	Lincoln	L	Y	4	Y	VC+	Working as social media specialist for nonprofit organization; not working in a STEM field although graduated with a STEM degree

*In this table, L = Latino/a, B = Black, W = White, and A = Asian American.

** Selectivity category index adapted from Barron's 2013 Index of College Selectivity (MC = Most Competitive; HC+ = Highly Competitive; HC = Highly Competitive; VC+ = Very Competitive+; VC = Very Competitive; C = Competitive; NR = Not Ranked (4-year colleges not ranked in Barron's 2013 Profiles of American Colleges, including all 2-year institutions). For the purposes of this study, the "top" category includes MC, HC+, HC, VC+, and VC schools.

attended a VC school and earned an MBA in health administration and became a Fellow at Sloan Kettering. Sokhem, an Asian American male from Southside, attended a two-year NR college and completed an associate's degree in computer network technology and was working as an IT specialist for a digital company; Padma, an Asian American female from Pella, completed a BA at a VC+ college and was pursuing graduate work in public health. In addition, Patricia, a Latina from Pella, did not earn a STEM degree but attended a VC college and became a community health worker. These students and others from Pella, Chavez, and Southside were also on their way into professional jobs or postgraduate training. Many continued to pursue STEM fields.

Most of the focal students from Buffalo in the follow-up group look somewhat different. Robert, a White male from STEM Academy who graduated from a VC college, was working as a roofer; Matthew, a White male from Global Horizons graduated from a C-level four-year college and owned his own construction business; and Sadie, a Latina from Lincoln who graduated from a VC+ college, became a social media specialist for a non–STEM-related organization in the not-for-profit sector (while Sadie graduated with a STEM degree, she was not working in that field after graduation). Isaac, a Black male from STEM Academy who graduated from a VC, was the only student among the Buffalo follow-up sample to complete a four-year STEM degree (math) *and* work in a STEM field (as a math teacher).

Among Buffalo two-year college graduates who majored in STEM, Jayme, a Black female from STEM Academy, completed a two-year degree in digital media and was pursuing a four-year degree in digital communications at a VC+ college; Mya, a female of Vietnamese origin from Global Horizons, finished a degree in nursing at a two-year NR college and was working as a nurse; Sarah, also from Global Horizons and of Vietnamese origin, completed a degree in nursing at a two-year NR college, continued her education to obtain additional certification as a medical assistant, and became a practicing nurse; Sofian, a male of Middle Eastern background from Global Horizons, received a degree in radiologic technology from a two-year NR college and was working as a radiology technician. No other Buffalo student who graduated in STEM was currently pursuing post-undergraduate work at a degree-granting institution in STEM.

In sum, an appreciably higher proportion of students in the Denver follow-up group, as opposed to those in Buffalo, graduated from a four-year college in STEM *and* were currently working in a STEM field or pursuing additional STEM education via an advanced certificate or graduate work as of 2019. They also attended and graduated from more highly ranked postsecondary institutions. Some were pursuing high-level postgraduate education in STEM, including a PhD or MD at very prestigious universities. Buffalo students were more likely to attend and graduate from a two-year school or a less highly ranked four-year school. In comparison to former Denver students, a very small number of former Buffalo students were working in STEM fields or pursuing additional STEM education in the four-year or two-year sector.

In light of this pattern, it is also interesting to note that the percentage of follow-up students in each city who *did not* graduate from *any* postsecondary institution—four or two year—is somewhat higher in Denver than Buffalo when Capital is removed from the analysis (see tables 6.1 and 6.2). Overall in Denver, 30 percent (eleven of thirty-seven) of follow-up students from the four sampled high schools failed to graduate from a four- or two-year college. But when Capital is removed from the analysis, 42 percent (eleven of twenty-six participants) of Denver students did not graduate from college, four or two year. In Buffalo, the undifferentiated noncollege graduation rate (students graduated from *neither* a four- nor two-year institution) across the four schools is 38 percent (ten of twenty-six students). These percentages across the two cities reflect the fact that *a somewhat higher proportion of Denver students who matriculated at a two-year school did not finish their degree.* This is not in evidence in Buffalo, where more students entered and graduated from a two-year school and were working in STEM fields or pursuing further education, often in STEM.

The important role of the two-year institution among Buffalo STEM graduates, as compelling as it may be, should not, however, overshadow the fact that former Denver students at all four schools were continuing to pursue STEM in postgraduate institutions to a notably greater extent than comparably capitalized former students in Buffalo. In this regard, a much higher proportion of former Denver students were on a path to higher-level STEM careers. Again, this is the case whether Capital is included in the analysis or not. Given comparable demographic backgrounds among focal students from seven of the eight schools, the findings cannot be explained by demographic characteristics.

To be clear, we are not suggesting that students who did not pursue STEM at four- or two-year institutions, or who were not employed in a STEM area, were not successful post-high school; this is not the case. What we are saying is that former Buffalo focal students who began high school with a stated interest in pursuing STEM in college and career (the majority of whom sustained this goal over the course of high school) were able to actualize this vision *to a lesser extent* than students of comparable demographic characteristics in Denver. This is especially notable because the current STEM education reform effort, particularly Inclusive STEM Schools (STEM schools with no criteria for admission; see chapter 1), aims to maximize STEM-related outcomes for low-income and minoritized students in college and career. As we see in this chapter, this happened to a far lesser extent in Buffalo than Denver. Even when a focal student did not pursue a four- or two-year degree in STEM, the likelihood of a Denver student continuing to pursue STEM in one form or another was greater. Pacco, for example, attended Denver's Pella High School—a school that, in contrast to Buffalo, offered a broader range of math and science courses and some counseling for college and career. Upon graduating from high school, Pacco entered the military, where he trained in aviation electronics technology. Although he does not appear in our table of STEM graduates as he did not receive a four- or two-year college degree, it is arguably the case that his exposure to math and science in high school positioned him to take advantage of STEM training in the military. Pacco continues to work as career military personnel in his now-chosen field, aviation technology. This is similarly the case for Patricia, also from Pella. Although she did not major in STEM at a four- or two-year college, she is currently practicing in a STEM field as a community health worker. It is arguably the case that capital she accrued in high school, unlike the "shadow capital" so evident in Buffalo, enabled her to position herself for and pursue this path.

Because Buffalo students were not scaffolded for STEM success in postsecondary institutions in the same way and to the same extent as those in Denver, it should come as no surprise that they had a more difficult time maximizing what they were exposed to by way of high school STEM courses and experiences. Put another way, accumulated knowledge and experiences embedded in schools must be such that they can be *activated* moving forward; that is, strategically deployed so that an individual can enter and be successful at the next higher level, within educational institutions and as well as the occupational sector. High schools cannot predominantly offer "shadow STEM capital," such as was the case in Buffalo, as discussed in chapter 3, and expect such capital to have the same level of strategic value and marketability moving forward as STEM capital that enables students to be successful in STEM courses as they become more advanced and more difficult. As we see in this chapter, Denver students in our study were more successful in this regard.

Importantly, our multiyear follow-up data make clear that the degree of erosion with respect to the initial vision for STEM reform for underrepresented minoritized students, coupled with substitution of shadow capital for more authentic STEM capital, had short- and long-term consequences. In point of fact, and as we see in this chapter, relatively small advantages, disadvantages, and consequences embedded within STEM opportunity structures and interpretive discourses in the two cities *compounded* moving forward. Although the within-school *mechanisms* that derailed an even envisioned broadening of opportunities (much less creating them) were largely the same in the two cities, the depth, nature, and short- and likely long-term impact of such derailment was different, with Buffalo students being left further and further behind. We will return to this point in the final chapter.

EFFECTIVELY MAINTAINED INEQUALITY

As we see in this chapter, it is with regard to *qualitative* distinctions in institutions from which largely similarly capitalized students in the two cities graduated—both at the high school and college levels—that differences in STEM trajectories become most apparent. In light of our findings, it is arguably the case that unrealized curricular enhancements in STEM for low-income and underrepresented minoritized students, particularly in Buffalo, unwittingly contributed to what Samuel Lucas calls "effectively maintained inequality."[10] At a general level, effectively maintained inequality recognizes that expansion of educational opportunities at any given level, in this case in STEM, is often accompanied by increasing institutional differentiation or heightened internal systemic stratification, thereby rendering the status of any given institution within a range of hierarchically possible options increasingly important. In the case at hand, although both cities made strides toward offering STEM opportunities for low-income and minoritized students, the fact that students at the Denver schools were better positioned to take advantage of more highly ranked undergraduate institutions and STEM degree programs means that Buffalo students were at an *increasing disadvantage* to compete for postgraduate opportunities and associated career outcomes. Put simply, what Buffalo students were offered by way of STEM courses and experiences in high school, coupled with the quality (competitiveness) of the undergraduate degree-granting institutions in STEM that students graduated from, increasingly made a difference with regard to one's future in the field. In spite of initially comparable stated and enacted attempts to broaden STEM opportunities for a largely comparable group of low-income and minoritized students in each city, we witnessed the accumulation of relative advantages and disadvantages between the two cities over time.

While it certainly has always been the case that students attend postsecondary institutions with varying degrees of power with respect to entrance to graduate school and professional career, this situation takes on heightened importance in a time of *effectively maintained inequality*, in which the question of *where* one goes to high school, college, and beyond, and in this case *where* one earns one's STEM degree, becomes increasingly important with regard to outcomes of interest. As we see here, a notable proportion of Denver students were able to capitalize on prior scaffolding in STEM to a much greater extent than students in Buffalo, as they transitioned into colleges and pursued and earned STEM degrees. It appears that the effective accumulation and deployment of authentic rather than "shadow" STEM capital, coupled with a somewhat more dependable identity as a person "good in STEM," propelled more Denver students toward higher-level postsecondary opportunities and STEM careers. We will discuss this latter point in chapter 8.

CHAPTER 7

A Closer Look at
STEM Trajectories in Denver

In this chapter we take a closer look at the subset of focal students in the follow-up group from Denver who finished high school and began college intending to major in a STEM field. These students were able to capitalize on their intent to pursue STEM in college, despite the limitations of their high schools' opportunity structures and figured worlds. We trace these students' "trajectories of identification" as they moved through high school and into and through college.[1]

By trajectories of identification we mean the course of the students' STEM-related experiences and identify formation constructed from semi-structured interviews and individual surveys. Interviews and surveys took place regularly from fall 2010, when the students were high school sophomores, through spring 2015, when they were finishing their second year of college, and then again in 2019. Among the focal students in Denver, we know that twenty-five began college intending to pursue STEM. They comprised 52 percent of our original Denver sample (twenty-five of forty-eight) and 68 percent of our Denver follow-up group (twenty-five of thirty-seven). Given that these students were not highly privileged—they represented marginalized groups, came from low- to modest-income families, and attended urban non-criterion public schools—the percentage pursuing some form of STEM in college was impressive. We identify common patterns in their high school to college trajectories and contrast them with other students in our Denver sample. Of special interest is how the system created by somewhat eroded opportunity structures and hollowed-out figured worlds in the Denver schools was overcome by a sizable number of Denver students.

We begin with the case of Sofia who, like nearly half of the students in our Denver sample, was identified and self-identified as high achieving in math after ninth grade but struggled to maintain that identity over the course of her high school career and did not choose to pursue STEM in college. With Sofia's case in mind, we then turn to the experiences of the twenty-five who began their college careers intending to major in STEM.

SOFIA'S CASE

Sofia is a Mexican American focal student from a low-income family who attended Southside High School in Denver.[2] As a tenth grader, she identified herself as someone who had always been good at math. She said at the time, "I've always liked [math]; when I have homework, that's the first thing I do, and then I always like going to my classes even though sometimes I haven't liked the teachers or something, but [math's] really fun, I like doing it." She said that math was her favorite subject. Her math grades had been mostly A's throughout her school life to that point. She reported that her ninth-grade math teacher recommended her for Honors Algebra II in tenth grade, and she did well and really liked that class. She planned to be ready to take Calculus in her senior year: "Since freshman year I told my counselor that I wanted to get to that Calculus." In eleventh grade, with her math teacher's recommendation, she enrolled in Honors Precalculus, along with three AP courses (AP Physics, AP Language Arts, and AP Spanish).

In Honors Precalculus, Sofia struggled, for the first time in her school career, to do well in math. She was not alone; many of the focal students in our study found themselves in the same situation. Their identities as "really good in math" (or science), as promoted by the school's figured world of "being good at math," suffered a blow during eleventh grade as the students began to take more advanced courses. Although Sofia's placement in the most advanced eleventh-grade math course at first reinforced her "good-at-math" identity, she soon found the coursework difficult and more time-consuming than before. It was no longer "easy"; she no longer "just got it"; she could no longer do the work quickly and on her own. Her math grades fell from 3.5 (of 4) at the end of tenth grade to 1.3 after the first semester of eleventh grade. Further, her relationships with her teachers changed, and her sense of herself was disrupted. Near the end of that year, Sofia told us:

> I was once the [math] teacher's pet, but not anymore, because they think I'm being disobedient to them. I have so much stuff to do, and I get it done, but just not on time, so they think I have something against them, but I don't. They think I don't have interest in school. . . . Last year I would just hear whatever we had to hear in the class. And I would take the quiz, and I would ace it. And now I actually have to study and do research on my own, and do my own practices. And *maybe* I could get a good score.

As a consequence of her struggle to do well in math, Sofia believed that she had become a "bad person"—disobedient and disrespectful—in the eyes of her teachers. As Sofia completed eleventh grade and moved on to twelfth grade, she lost confidence in being a good student and a good person. She began to narrate herself in mostly negative terms. Instead of talking about her accomplishments, she talked about no longer being "the best," no longer being "at the top," no longer being "a star," and how much "better" other students were doing than she. She said teachers and counselors gave those students all the attention and praise. Sofia and other focal students like her seemed to find themselves at a loss for how to move on, both discursively and performatively. At Chavez, students who struggled in advanced math accused formerly supportive teachers and counselors of ignoring their interests in going to college and focusing only on students who were "doing better," that is, those who could continue to perform the classwork consistent with the figured world of being good at math.

In Sofia's case, her math grades recovered somewhat in twelfth grade, but she was not satisfied with them. She pronounced AP Calculus her "least favorite class" because "it's so hard to understand" and "it consumes a lot of my time."

Sofia also lost confidence in her plan for the future. As long as she was good in math (through tenth grade), she thought she would like to become an architect or a doctor because, as she said, "both involve math." By the end of eleventh grade, she was thinking about becoming a psychologist. At the end of twelfth grade, she told us she planned to pursue a pre-med degree, at the same time admitting that she no longer liked math, and science had always been her hardest and weakest subject.

Some focal students who struggled with more advanced math or science coursework in eleventh or twelfth grade affiliated with another school subject in which their grades remained high—for example, in history or English literature—and then chose that field to pursue in college. Others, like Sofia, could not seem to find their footing and, like her, halfheartedly named a major they already did not like or did not expect to do well in. When Sofia began college, she designated her major as "undecided" and later chose early education.

The math knowledge and skills that Sofia exhibited and that contributed to her earlier identity as accomplished in math and as a morally good person were consistent with a symbolic logic that celebrated students who found their work easy, could do it quickly, and could make the highest grades. In the context of her school, Sofia did what she was expected to do, especially in math. She strived to do well in classes, follow the rules, make good grades, push herself to take advanced courses, prepare for college, and choose a promising career path, such as in math. But as she approached high school graduation, she could not maintain the "good student" identity in math that had sustained and motivated her through most of her years in school and that she had come to expect of herself. She graduated from high school with a dubious commitment to next steps.

MATH AND SCIENCE SUCCESS STORIES

Many who have written about underrepresented students who succeed in math or science subjects, degree programs, or careers stress the importance of developing a strong identity in a STEM field.[3] This strong identity has been defined by Ebony Omotola McGee as an internal focus on enjoying and embracing mathematics (or science) and "a passion for mathematics and engineering" (or science).[4] Others refer to this as intrinsic motivation or "finding something inherently interesting or enjoyable."[5] According to McGee, a strong identity rooted in this passion for STEM subject matter includes coping strategies for withstanding racist and sexist attacks on one's interest and competence in these fields.

Most of the students in our full sample did not talk about being intrinsically motivated by subject matter per se. A primary motivation to continue in these subject areas was the social approbation of being recognized as "good" in the math or science of the courses they took and in terms of the figured world that circulated about these subject areas in their schools. When a student could no longer sustain a good-in-math or good-in-science identity in the school's social and cultural context, as happened to Sofia, motivation to continue in math or science was threatened and could fade. What is impressive—given the somewhat restricted opportunity structures and hollowed-out figured worlds these students experienced in Denver—is that some of them did succeed in STEM into and through college.

Tables 7.1 and 7.2 display the characteristics and outline the trajectories of the twenty-five Denver students who continued to pursue some kind of STEM beyond high school. Their interests and experiences are varied, and no one pattern holds true for all. In the sections that follow, we discuss in more detail the trajectories of these focal students toward a degree in STEM and the similarities and differences among the cases.

Table 7.1 includes the demographic characteristics of the twenty-five Denver focal students who entered college planning to major in STEM. It also shows the trajectories of intended college majors named by these focal students from tenth to twelfth grade in high school and as they headed to college. The type and competitiveness of the college each student attended is also indicated.

Several things stand out in table 7.1. First, the students were quite consistent in their choice of major over the period from tenth grade to the start of college. Although some of the labels for majors became more specific over time, the students' subject matter interests were surprisingly stable. This was the case regardless of high school attended,

TABLE 7.1 Focal students continuing in math or science into college, Denver

(n = 25)

NAME	SCHOOL	RACE/ETHNICITY	M/F	GRADE 10 INTENDED MAJOR/JOB	GRADE 11 INTENDED MAJOR/JOB	GRADE 12 INTENDED MAJOR/JOB	SELECTIVITY CATEGORY INDEX**	ENTERING COLLEGE MAJOR
*Alice	Chavez (STEM)	Latina	F	Vet	Vet	Vet	VC (4 year)	Pre-vet
*Ana	Chavez (STEM)	Latina	F	Math, orthodontics	Orthodontics, massage therapy	Sports medicine	C (4 year)	Health and exercise science
*Adriana	Chavez (STEM)	Latina	F	Pediatric medicine, business	Pediatric medicine	Biology/premed	VC (4 year)	Biology/premed
*Anne	Chavez (STEM)	White	F	Neurosurgeon	Medicine	Nursing	NR (2 year)	Nursing
Alfonso	Chavez (STEM)	Latino	M	Engineering	Criminal justice	Automotive engineering	NR (4 year)	Engineering
Alma	Chavez (STEM)	Latina	F	Math	Math, computers	Engineering, nursing	NR (4 year)	Nursing
*Padma	Pella (STEM)	Asian	F	Science	Biochemistry, nursing	Biology, premed	VC+ (4 year)	Biology, premed
*Penny	Pella (STEM)	White	F	Don't know	Biology, engineering	Math/education	NR (4 year)	Math/education
*Pahal	Pella (STEM)	Asian	F	Premed	Premed	Premed	VC (4 year)	Premed
*Prak	Pella (STEM)	Asian	M	Biology	Biology	Biology	VC (4 year)	Biology
Pedro	Pella (STEM)	Latino	M	Engineering	Aerospace engineering	Aerospace engineering	VC (4 year)	Engineering
Selena	Southside	Latina	F	Pediatric medicine	Pediatric medicine	Biology/premed	HC (4 year)	Biology/education
*Sokhem	Southside	Asian	M	Engineering	Engineering	Electrician	NR (2 year)	Undecided/engineer?

TABLE 7.1 *Continued*

(*n* = 25)

NAME	SCHOOL	RACE/ETHNICITY	M/F	GRADE 10 INTENDED MAJOR/JOB	GRADE 11 INTENDED MAJOR/JOB	GRADE 12 INTENDED MAJOR/JOB	SELECTIVITY CATEGORY INDEX**	ENTERING COLLEGE MAJOR
Stefan	Southside	Latino	M	Engineering	Mechanical engineering	Engineering	NR (2 year)	Engineering
Samy	Southside	Latino	M	Engineering	Not enrolled	Engineering	NR (2 year)	Engineering
*Candalaria	Capital	Latina	F	Premed	Premed	Undecided	HC+ (4 year)	Undecided, something medical
*César	Capital	Latino	M	Undecided	Biology, political science	Undecided	HC+ (4 year)	Undecided, something medical
*Chang	Capital	Asian	F	Math teacher, engineer, physicist	Speech pathology, music	Speech pathology, music	VC (4 year)	Speech pathology and audiology, music
*Catherine	Capital	Black	F	Engineering or biochemistry	Business, psychology	Engineering	VC (4 year)	Chemical engineering
*Carlos	Capital	Latino	M	Psychology	Neuroscience	Neuroscience	VC (4 year)	Neuroscience/premed
*Chaquille	Capital	Black/White	M	Music	Music, business	Music, computer science	MC (4 year)	Computer science, music
*Chandra	Capital	Black	F	Engineering	Engineering	Engineering	VC (4 year)	Mechanical engineering
*Cailey	Capital	Black	F	Pre-vet	Pre-vet	Pre-vet	C (4 year)	Zoology, psychology
*Carolynne	Capital	Black	F	Engineering, premed	Premed, biological research	Engineering, premed	VC+ (4 year)	Biology
Charles	Capital	White	M	Premed	Premed	Premed	VC (4 year)	Biology

*Those who graduated from college in STEM, *n* = 18 or 72%; see also table 7.2.

**Selectivity category index adapted from Barron's 2013 Index of College Selectivity (MC = Most Competitive; HC+ = Highly Competitive+; HC = Highly Competitive; VC+ = Very Competitive+; VC = Very Competitive; C = Competitive; NR = Not Ranked (4-year colleges not ranked in Barron's 2013 Profiles of American Colleges, including all 2-year institutions).

TABLE 7.2 *STEM college and employment outcomes for focal students who pursued STEM into college (italic indicates STEM major or employment), Denver*

NAME	HIGH SCHOOL	RACE/ETHNICITY	M/F	MAJOR IN 2ND YEAR OF COLLEGE (2015)	COLLEGE GRADUATE?	FINAL COLLEGE MAJOR	EDUCATION/EMPLOYMENT BEYOND FIRST BACHELOR'S DEGREE
Alice	Chavez (STEM)	Latina	F	*Pre-vet*	Y	Medical assistant	
Ana	Chavez (STEM)	Latina	F	Health and exercise science	Y	Health and exercise science	
Adriana	Chavez (STEM)	Latina	F	Nursing	Y	Nursing	Nursing assistant
Anne	Chavez (STEM)	White	F	Para-medicine	Y	Para-medicine	
Alfonso	Chavez (STEM)	Latino	M	Criminal justice	Y	Criminal justice	Student advisor
Alma	Chavez (STEM)	Latina	F	Nursing	Y	Social work	
Padma	Pella (STEM)	Asian	F	*Biology*	Y	*Biology*	*Working on MA in public health*
Penny	Pella (STEM)	White	F	*Math education*	Y	*Math education*	
Pahal	Pella (STEM)	Asian	F	*Premed*	Y	*Premed*	
Prak	Pella (STEM)	Asian	M	*Biology*	Y	*Biology*	*MBA in health administration, Fellow at Sloan Kettering*
Pedro	Pella (STEM)	Latino	M	*Computer science*	Unknown	Unknown	

TABLE 7.2 *Continued*

NAME	HIGH SCHOOL	RACE/ETHNICITY	M/F	MAJOR IN 2ND YEAR OF COLLEGE (2015)	COLLEGE GRADUATE?	FINAL COLLEGE MAJOR	EDUCATION/EMPLOYMENT BEYOND FIRST BACHELOR'S DEGREE
Selena	Southside	Latina	F	Biology	Y	Psychology, but knew before graduating that she wanted nursing	Nursing (2nd) BA
Sokhem	Southside	Asian	M	Computer technology	Y	Computer technology	IT specialist
Stefan	Southside	Latino	M	Engineering	Unknown	Unknown	
Samy	Southside	Latino	M	Engineering	Unknown	Unknown	
Candalaria	Capital	Latina	F	Neuroscience	Y	Neuroscience	Working as medical assistant, studying for MCAT
César	Capital	Latino	M	Biology	Y	Biology	
Chang	Capital	Asian	F	Speech pathology and audiology	Y	Speech and language pathology	Working on MA in speech and language pathology
Catherine	Capital	Black	F	Chemical engineering	Y	Chemical engineering	Working on PhD in toxicology
Carlos	Capital	Latino	M	Neuroscience and psychology	Y	Neuroscience and psychology	Math teacher
Chaquille	Capital	Black/White	M	Music, computer science	Y	Music, computer science	Software engineer
Chandra	Capital	Black	F	Electrical engineering	Y	Electrical engineering	Working in engineering
Cailey	Capital	Black	F	Psychology, minor in zoology	Y	Health and exercise science	Working on MA in neurogenetics
Carolynne	Capital	Black	F	Biology	Y	Biology	
Charles	Capital	White	M	Theater	Y	Theater	

Note: n = 19 who completed college with a STEM major as of 2019 (including Selena, who got a 2nd BA in STEM); n = 3 who completed college with a non-STEM major as of 2019; n = 3 for whom we could not obtain information in 2019.

race/ethnicity, or gender. It is also impressive to see the number of girls in this group: girls were better represented than boys among Denver focal students who continued in STEM (fifteen girls, 10 boys), although girls were only slightly overrepresented among the focal students as a whole (see table 1.1 in chapter 1). Another finding is that White focal students were underrepresented among this group, while Black focal students were overrepresented. This result may be due in part to our efforts to over-sample underrepresented minoritized students when selecting schools and focal students at the beginning of our study. To be clear, however, although an interesting finding, we cannot definitely account for the overrepresentation of girls *or* minoritized students among those whose subject matter interests in STEM were stable relative to those of other groups (nonminoritized students and males). Also evident in table 7.1 is the overrepresentation of focal students from Capital. Ten of twenty-five focal students (40 percent) who went on to college intending to major in STEM were from Capital.

Table 7.2 extends the timeline for the Denver focal students who started college in STEM to show the trajectories of STEM majors during college and at graduation. We verified that nineteen of the twenty-five focal students (76 percent) who said they intended to major in a STEM field when they entered college continued in STEM and graduated with a major in a STEM field.[6] This, too, is a surprising finding in light of previous research on the underrepresentation of students like those in our study in STEM. As in table 7.1, Capital stood out again: nine of the nineteen focal students (47 percent) who finished college with a STEM degree had attended Capital. However, it is important to remember that the students at Capital, all of whom attended four-year colleges, were easier to find in college graduation records than those who attended two-year schools. Additionally, those with an online presence, also more common among Capital students, were easier to find than those without.

The data in table 7.2 confirm the stability of these students' interests in STEM through high school and into college, despite the challenging conditions at three of the four Denver schools that reduced opportunities for advanced STEM coursework, eliminated STEM academies, and diverted college guidance counselors to record-keeping tasks.

Somehow these students overcame the limitations that we found in their schools. The data also highlight the impressive college and career pathways that the focal students embarked on, including students from Southside, Chavez, and Pella who were not privileged in the same way as those at Capital and certainly not in the ways described for students at Forestview in Buffalo and other middle-, upper-middle, and upper-class public and private institutions in the United States.[7] These strikingly positive outcomes challenged us to examine the individual cases of these successful students.

ADVANCEMENT IN STEM OVER TIME

As we closely examine the experiences of the students who pursued STEM into college, we illustrate how these students developed and sustained trajectories of identification in STEM fields. During grade 10, all nineteen students who graduated from college in STEM identified themselves with reference to the figured world of being good in math or science as discussed in chapter 5. The majority (thirteen of nineteen) described themselves as exemplars of the figured world: being "really good" at math or science and really liking one or both fields because "it comes easily," "I just get it," and "I make really good grades." Three others made repeated positive references to the figured world but did not think they personally measured up. Nonetheless, these three expressed deep interests in math or science, similar to the successful undergraduates that McGee studied.[8] The other three rejected the figured world as meaningful to them and pursued math or science on their own terms.

Personifying the Figured World of "Being Good" in Math or Science

Cailey (Capital) was one girl who identified closely with the figured world: "I'm really strong in math and physics because everything they've brought up, I've already known. My grades are great. I like the stuff I know how to do—math and science are my best." Another was Selena (Southside), who told us: "I'm good at most things, and I'm *really* good in math and science. Math is my very favorite subject; it just comes easily to me."[9] Another was Chandra (Capital), who said: "I just really like math. I could not do anything in class and then the week of the test, I start focusing and learn everything in a week. It just comes really easily to me." Another was Chang: "My strengths are math. I used to be really amazing in science, but it's become hard. Honors Biology was really hard [she made a C+]; I just did not understand what was happening. But when it [involves] math, like Honors Chemistry, then I'm still really good at it, and I really like it" [she made a B+]. Another was Ana (Chavez), who had the following to say when asked by a researcher:

RESEARCHER: What makes you think you are strong in math?
ANA: Just because I get it easily [she got an A].
RESEARCHER: Do you have any idea at this point what you might major in in college?
ANA: Math, because I just get it.

These students contrasted their strengths in math or science with weaknesses they believed they had in language arts. A common complaint was that "there are no right answers" in language arts, "which drives me crazy." Cailey explained, "Like in some of my classes we have to write essays, and I always have to go back and revise it like three thousand times before I officially get it right." Selena complained that she often struggled to identify the "meaning" in a text, and even when she did, it was not the meaning her teacher *wanted* (emphasis ours). Padma (Pella) told us: "My weakness is language arts because English is so complicated, especially the grammar—it's so difficult. And trying to analyze the author's point of view, there's no right answer. It's so complicated. In science you know the right way to do things . . . You don't have that in literature. You can't learn from your mistakes, because there's so many possibilities."[10]

Deep Interest in Subject Matter

In grade 10, three of the nineteen students allowed that they did not meet the model of "being good" in math or science, but they really wanted to pursue a STEM field anyway. Carolynne (Capital) said, "I don't get the best grades in math or science, but it's really, really what

I want to do." Catherine (Capital) had a similar view: "I work hard and I always try, even if I don't get the best grades. I just like math so much and really want to understand it. That's what keeps me coming in everyday for extra help." Padma (Pella) expressed a similar view: "I don't make the best grades [in science], and I know I should spend more time studying. But I have such a deep interest in science, and that's what I want to major in in college." Later, in eleventh grade, she complained about struggling in Chemistry and needing to get help from her teacher, but went on to say that she was really interested in chemistry and would probably choose it as a college major. The deep interests these three students expressed are reminiscent of Ebony McGee's argument that "passion" for the subject matter is a critical element for underrepresented students who pursue STEM.

"Working the System"

The three other students (all boys) described themselves as rejecting the figured world of being good in math/science, but each did so in a different way. Chaquille (Capital), for example, described his math and science classes as "easy, and I know how to get an A . . . It doesn't really take much. Like in math, I can get very, very good grades [because] I start to observe the patterns, then I can do things in a way that makes it look really impressive, when it's really not." In the dialogue that followed, the researcher asked:

> RESEARCHER: Would you say you're really good in math or science?
> CHAQUILLE: No, not at all. There's nothing really special about these advanced courses. A lot of kids are perfectly mentally capable of doing the [advanced] math I am doing right now. It's just bragging rights to say, 'I'm in Calculus or I'm in honors.' And it looks good for colleges."

For Chaquille, the model of being good at math or science at his school was not compelling and did not impress him. He could demonstrate it, but he did so in a cynical way and as a means of getting into a "good" college.

Carlos (Capital), too, was dismissive of the figured world of being good in math or science at his school. He said, "Being good in math and science at this school is just memorization and test taking." But he said he liked math because "it's figuring out complex problems that others find hard, and it's really easy for me." In science, he said he just writes down whatever the teacher says and doesn't have any problem retaining the information without studying. "There wasn't anything in math or science that I really didn't understand. Looking back, it was generally pretty easy." He called what he did "working the system"—that is, making good grades by figuring out "what each teacher really cares about" (homework, class participation) and organizing his time and effort accordingly.

Sokhem (Southside), the third student in this group, seemed to reject the whole idea of high school as a place to learn important things. He believed that he was "really good at math" because friends asked him for help with it, and his math teachers liked him. He knew he had received a very high score on his grade 9 state standardized test in math (hence his inclusion in our study). He believed he could understand the material simply by attending class and listening. He readily admitted that he did not turn in class assignments, never did the homework, and as a consequence, made low grades. His view was: "I already understand it. Why should I practice it? . . . If I hear something interesting in class, I go home and look it up on the internet—for more information." He talked frequently about "being friends" with his math teachers and "messing around with them in class." In one example, he reported having a contest with a math teacher to see who could answer 100 math questions the fastest: "So, it was timed. [The teacher] finished first, and I finished one second behind." He loved such contests and spoke of them often. He spoke favorably of teachers—in math, physics, civics, music, and history—who engaged with him in this type of "messing around." About one teacher, he said, "He and I had a tiny in-school agreement that as long as I do good on all his tests, he would still pass me with at least a C," even if he didn't do the in-class assignments or the homework and never took notes in class. Sokhem knew his grades were terrible (D average in math and science in high school), but he continued to think of himself as "smart in math and science," "able to figure out on my own" what he needed to know, and satisfied to spend time in classes where he could "mess around," including in math and science. Importantly, his teachers abetted his behavior and attitude by advancing him every year into a higher-level math and science course despite his very low grades and dismissive attitude about schoolwork.

A PIVOTAL TIME: ELEVENTH AND TWELFTH GRADES

For many of the students in our full sample, like Sofia, who was profiled at the beginning of this chapter, eleventh and twelfth grades were pivotal times when their understanding of themselves as "good" in math or science was challenged when they began to take more advanced and more difficult courses. For many, their math and science courses became honors, AP, or IB diploma courses. This was a moment when students who were identified as "good in" math or science and who had learned to identify that way began to question themselves as they struggled in advanced Precalculus, Calculus, Chemistry, or Physics. In Sofia's case, she lost confidence in her ability to be "good in math" and decided not to pursue it after high school.

Given the compromised opportunity structures, diverted counselors, and hollowed-out figured worlds that students experienced in our study schools, it is not surprising that more advanced and more difficult math and science classes would trip them up. Among the nineteen students who pursued math or science degrees after high school, many did struggle to maintain high grades in math or science during grades 11 and 12. But each found sources of support for their math and science identities, either in school or outside it. Selena provides one example.

Selena's Case

Selena (Southside) found Honors Physics in grade 11 harder than expected, and she struggled with the implications for her identity. For the first time, she complained that she had to work "really, really hard to keep up my grades" in science. She continued to do really well in math (Honors Precalculus), but she was surprised and unsettled by her experience in Physics. She wanted to do well in science in preparation for college (medical school). Worried that her high GPA was in jeopardy, she went to her physics teacher after class and asked for help. She had never had to do this before, and she was nervous. But she was pleasantly surprised to find her teacher welcoming and willing to work with her after school. She also got help from her AVID (Advancement Via Individual Determination) teacher (who provided college support at her school; see chapter 4) and ended the year with an A in Physics.[11] At the end of that year, Selena's physics teacher (a male) told us:

> PHYSICS TEACHER: She has done outstanding. She is one of the brighter, harder-working students in quite a while. And, she is quite aware of her limitations. She comes to me a lot, she gets help quite often. I have students who do this because of the grade, but she does it because she wants to learn it. We even had a discussion about it. She said, "Nobody is going to care about my grade in ten years. I want to learn this even though it's hard." She told me she'd be here often, and she was.
> RESEARCHER: Did you ever encourage her to pursue a STEM field?
> PHYSICS TEACHER: Oh, definitely. She told me she wants to be a doctor, and I said, "That's great!" I also told her that young Hispanic women in any science or technology field are rare and that she would be able to do great things.

During our interviews with Selena in twelfth grade, she mentioned her former physics teacher often. He became a mentor and a friend, and she later asked him to write her a letter of recommendation for college, which he did.

In twelfth grade, Selena took AP Calculus and AP Biology. This time she found herself struggling in Calculus (math). And this time she sounded even more desperate, and her grades fell more sharply. She reported (again) that she had never worked so hard, and "even when I studied really hard, I never understood what was going on. I asked my teacher for *anything* extra I could do, and it was really hard. It was a first-time thing where I had to try that hard." That year, her GPA in math fell from 5.2/A (AP Precalculus weighted more as an advanced course) to 3.5/B- (AP Calculus). She was deeply disappointed, but she kept at it: asking for help, doing extra work, and "working really, really hard." Selena had some other things going for her, too. She received a high ACT score (not outstanding but very good) and a high class ranking, and her teachers encouraged her to apply to competitive colleges. About this, she was obviously pleased: "They were talking to me about how I can go to a *really* good college, and like maybe outside of Colorado, and I kinda listened to them. And I couldn't really believe it." She did apply to competitive colleges and began her college career at a prestigious school with a full-ride scholarship and a plan to major in biology and become a doctor. Unfortunately, Selena became homesick and felt out of place at her first college. She transferred to a less prestigious college close to home and switched her major to psychology. Although she graduated with a degree in psychology, she told us that even before graduation, she knew she really wanted to pursue something in the medical field. Immediately after college graduation, she enrolled for a second undergraduate degree in nursing and subsequently graduated with a nursing degree.

Other Girls

Among the girls who went on to college in STEM, Selena's case illustrates a theme that appeared in the trajectories of the focal students who embraced the figured world of math or science at their schools and those who had a deep interest. Ana, Adriana, Alma, Anne, Chang, Chandra, Cailey, Catherine, Penny, and Padma all struggled to perform as well as they had come to expect in one or more of their math or science classes in grade 11 or 12. Their struggles shook their confidence in their sense of themselves as "good" or "good enough" in math or science but did not dissuade them from pursuing these fields. Like Selena, they found supportive teachers who worked with them individually. Ana, Adriana, Alma, and Anne got extra support from the AVID and Talent Search programs they participated in during high school (both programs were externally supported college preparatory programs offered at the school for underserved students; see chapter 4).[12] They were enrolled in AVID courses every year of high school, and the AVID teacher was a resource who reviewed classwork with them, provided in-class study time, encouraged them to meet with their regular teachers for extra help, helped them navigate the college application process, and served as an advocate for them in school. The Talent Search program supported college preparation and college visits. Chandra, Cailey, Catherine, and Padma got extra help from teachers and also participated in summer programs that introduced them to adults and older students with similar career interests. Chandra, with an interest in engineering but limited information about it, participated in free "engineering camps" each summer. She told us: "Those camps changed my perception of engineers. I was worried that an engineer was some White guy with glasses and pants pulled up high. But at camp, I learned that engineering was all about math and science where you're free to be creative and hands-on. That got me really interested." She continued, "The friends I made there, I could see myself doing that for the rest of my life!" Catherine, also interested in engineering, participated in summer programs organized by a Black professional association. Padma attended summer music programs (she played the cello) where she traveled to performances with older students who encouraged her by telling her what to expect in college and helped her with her college application essays.

For these students, including Selena, who had come to identify and be identified by others as "good" in math or science, it was very important to try and maintain this valued identity. We heard this in the students' repeated expressions of worries about their grades and their reports of working "really hard," needing and seeking extra help, and trying to take advantage of available resources and supports. Although the figured world of being good in math or science in the Denver schools we studied can be construed as "hollowed out," it nonetheless seemed to motivate these students to keep working hard and trying to do very well in their school math or science courses (such as they were) in order to preserve a valued identity. This is especially clear in contrast to Buffalo where the figured world of "passing" did not hold as much promise for the construction of an identity that could launch students into college trajectories in STEM. All of these Denver students graduated with an undergraduate degree in a STEM-related field and took jobs or pursued further education in these fields.

What About the Boys?

For Chaquille, Carlos, and Sokhem, who rejected the schools' figured world of being good at math or science, their experiences in eleventh and twelfth grades were different. Grades and class performance had little effect on them. In Chaquille's case, although his grades dipped slightly in eleventh grade Honors Physics, he never saw himself as struggling academically in high school. As he thought about college, he knew he wanted to pursue music in some way, but he was not sure he should major in music. He considered both business and computer science because, as he put it: "Music is a leap of faith in terms of whether you'll be successful or not. Computer engineering is not nearly as much a leap of faith as it is hard work. So, I'm caught between a secure job that I might not enjoy as much or an awesome job where I could wind up extremely unsuccessful." In senior year, he took AP Computer Science and decided against business. He had also become intrigued with the mathematics in computer science and its connections to music composition. He decided that he wanted to attend a university rather than a music conservatory so that he would have a chance to sample many different fields.

Chaquille was accepted with a full scholarship to a very prestigious college. He thought he would probably major in music and minor in computer science, which is what he did. Interestingly, when he started working, it was as a software engineer.

Carlos's GPA fell during high school, but it didn't concern him. He had been interested in psychology in tenth grade and then switched to neuroscience because "it's more prestigious than psychology." He said he had researched the field of neuroscience and was confident that it was what he wanted to do in college. His view was that his grades were sufficient to get him into a good college to study neuroscience, so there was no need to work any harder or try to get better grades in high school. He did receive a college degree in neuroscience. He did not become a neuroscientist, but he did stay in STEM and became a math teacher.

Sokhem's math and science grades were pretty terrible throughout high school, but he remained mostly unconcerned until the end of his senior year. In eleventh grade, he told us: "I know how to do everything. Homework is so pointless to me, so I don't do any homework. That's my own personal fault; I should have done it. But, senior year I'll be trying to do better because my classes aren't as difficult as this year, and I can bring [my GPA] up to a 2.8 [of 4]. I should be fine." He said he wanted to go to engineering school. In twelfth grade, he realized his grades weren't nearly good enough to get him into the four-year engineering school he wanted to attend. His new plan was to attend a community college for two years and become an electrician. Then he said, "I'll see if I still have the drive to become a civil engineer. If so, I'll transfer."

The end of high school was a sad time for Sokhem. He started to cry during the interview that took place then. "I know I messed up: I don't want to be where my dad is where he can't retire until he's extremely old. I don't want that." He said he had talked to one of this teachers: "When I informed her of my stepping-stone plan—electrician first, then civil engineer, she told me, 'You don't need a stepping-stone to where you're going. You could, if you were to truly attend and put real effort into your schoolwork, you could become a civil engineer in three years. As you are now, that might be an issue, but if you were to fight the other half of you now, you can do whatever you want. I can see that in you.'" Sokhem knew she meant he should fight his "lazy half," but he was never able to do that in high school. During his two years at the community college, Sokhem reported that he "loved the school" and that he was getting academic support from relatives and professors there. He had also decided to pursue computer technology, which is what he did in college and as a job after college.

As discussed earlier in this chapter, the boys in our follow-up sample from Denver who later pursued STEM in college seemed to reject the figured world of "being good" in math or science that circulated in their high schools. Nonetheless, they continued in STEM fields. Unlike the girls, they did not seem to worry about any increasing difficulty with math or science coursework over time or low grades in these courses. At least in their presentations to us, they seemed to believe that high school was rather inconsequential for their future, except as a means to get into college.[13] This gender difference among a particularly located low-income group of largely underrepresented students is a topic beyond the scope of our study. Like many insights gleaned from our ten-year investigation, this issue warrants further research.

A PIVOTAL MOMENT: DECIDING ON A COLLEGE MAJOR

At one time or another, all the students who eventually went on to pursue math or science expressed anxieties about going to college. Their concerns included whether they would "stand out" as college applicants, whether they would get into a desired college, how they would pay for college, where they would live (on campus or at home), and how hard college work would be. A big source of anxiety was what to choose as a college major. This issue became especially salient in grades 11 and 12. Penny, in grade 11, told us anxiously: "I just don't know what any of them [majors, careers] are; I need to know more about my options. I wish I knew more about engineering. I would like to know more about it, you know, because I want to make sure that what I'm doing is what makes me happy. I don't want to get into something I won't like." Alma, in grade 11, had similar concerns. She said she didn't know what to major in or how to figure it out: "I really like the [engineering] thing. I was thinking something about computers, but I just wasn't sure. I just want something with computers, you know, with math involved. But I'm not sure. I don't know how to be sure." Given Penny's uncertainty, her plan at the time was to go to a noncompetitive local college and see whether she could figure out what she really wanted to do there. Later she told us she was thinking of "a few majors"—"smaller ones like cosmetology that are faster to graduate, and bigger ones like engineering. I'm just not sure." And she said: "I really do want to go to college. What's hard is choosing what I really want." Catherine said: "I got all A's last year, but this year it has been hard keeping that drive when you don't know what you want to do. If I could narrow down the school I want to go to and the program I want, I could be more focused. I want a job I will love, where I can wake up every morning and say, 'I love my job.' It's really bothering me [not to know]."

Like Selena and Chaquille, many were concerned about making a "practical" choice of major in addition to other considerations. Assurance that a job would be available after college was crucial to making a practical choice. In tenth grade, Anne talked about wanting to become a neurosurgeon so that she could help other people with a medical condition she had. She expressed disappointment that her own neurosurgeon "didn't communicate very well" about her disability or her options. She wanted to contribute in that field and do a better job. As a senior, she reported researching the field and discovering that she would have to train to be a neurosurgeon first, before she could specialize in the area of her disability. She said, "I want to go straight to the specialty." So, she decided on nursing: "Nursing is the kind of thing where you know you're going to be able to be employed afterwards, and you'll be able to pay off your loans." Similarly, Ana aspired to become an orthodontist in tenth and eleventh grades ("it's better than a dentist, because you make more money") but decided against it: "I found out that orthodontist would take about 12 years, and it's like going to school all over again, and I didn't want that . . . Four [more] years [of college] would be the most."

At Southside, Chavez, and Pella, deciding on a major was a fraught affair for students as they approached high school graduation. This is not surprising given the limited counseling available to high-achieving students at their schools. Even at Capital, where students received considerably more college and career counseling, focal students expressed concern about choosing a major. Many felt strongly that they did not have sufficient information about college majors and what that might lead to in terms of a job after college. They also felt that this information was "very important" in choosing a college major. Another important consideration for these students was to select a major that would lead to a job that would keep them close to family. Selecting a college major was not only about pursuing a field of interest; it was also about not taking a lot of time, not costing a lot of money, getting a good job, and staying close to home.

During the focal students' twelfth-grade year (2013), we developed a job outlook survey for them and their parents. The survey listed titles of job categories expected to increase by at least 20 percent in Colorado during the next five years; that is, these were jobs, relatively close to home, that were expected to have high availability for students graduating from college at that time.[14] On the survey, respondents were asked to indicate whether they knew anyone who held each job type and whether they thought they (or their daughter or son) would be good at that job. There were eighteen job categories on the list. Most of them involve STEM. The job categories were:

Forensic Science Technicians	Environmental Scientists and Engineers
Health Educators	Biological Technicians
Medical and Health Service Managers	Athletic Trainers
Conservation Scientists	Interpreters and Translators
Air Traffic Controllers	Cardiovascular Technicians
Physical Therapists	Radiation Therapists
Respiratory Therapists	Registered Nurses
Veterinary Technicians	Dental Hygienists
Environmental and Health Science Technicians	Forest and Conservation Technicians

Surprisingly, because this list of job categories was available to students, parents, and counselors on the *College in Colorado* website (see chapter 4), neither students nor parents surveyed said they were familiar with more than a few of these job categories. Only four categories— Interpreters and Translators, Physical Therapists, Dental Hygienists, and Registered Nurses—were familiar to most, and only nursing was selected as an intended major at the end of high school by any of the Denver focal students in our study. Thus, it seems that although students expressed considerable anxiety about what to choose as a college major, how to pursue it efficiently, how to tie it reliably to the job market, and how to remain close to family in the long run, they apparently did not, for whatever reason, know about or consider relevant information that was available to them.

SERENDIPITOUS ENCOUNTERS

Several students who were considering various majors had serendipitous experiences near the end of high school that contributed to their decision regarding an appropriate major. Catherine at Capital, who worried that she didn't know what she really wanted to do in college, discovered a topic in AP Calculus her senior year that really excited her (previously she had wondered whether she should major in business or psychology): "We started doing these revolutions about the y- and x-axis. So, if you look at a graph, if you take a three-dimensional shape—like a cone or a cup—and you want to know the volume, you can put it on a graph and you can calculate the volume from revolving it around an x- or y-axis! It was a really hard math concept, but it was also really exciting! So, I started thinking, 'Where can I do this all the time? If I want to do this kind of math, where can I do it?'" Later she reported getting some basic books about it, and she exclaimed, "Now I want to be about solving problems all day using math and physics!"

Chang had a strong interest in vocal music. During her junior year, she expressed the view that math was very important in music theory, especially if she wanted to become a conductor. As a junior, she became interested in speech pathology because "it's about how things come out and what happens, and because it involves helping people." She attributed this interest to a casual conversation she had with a stranger on the bus. She went on, "And ever since then, it's been locked in." She chose speech pathology as her major in college.

Ana at Chavez had always loved math but did not like science. In tenth grade she wanted to become an orthodontist because "they make good money," but then she decided it required too much schooling for her. In eleventh grade she was thinking about becoming a massage therapist because "I enjoy giving massages to my basketball teammates." Then in twelfth grade she changed her mind about science ("now I like it") and thought she might want to become an athletic trainer or go into sports medicine. She attributed her new interest in science to her twelfth-grade class, Anatomy and Physiology. She spent time talking with the teacher about the class and career options. The teacher told her she would have more options and make more money in sports medicine than as an athletic trainer. On the spot, Ana said she decided to major in sports medicine (the program was called Health and Exercise Science at her college).

By the time they were approaching the end of high school, these three students, and perhaps others, had acquired some knowledge of fields that interested them such that specific activities, discussions with teachers, or chance encounters could solidify a decision about a college major. An important point here is that these students knew enough about the disciplines that they were thinking of pursuing to engage in thoughtful consideration and discussion of a range of college majors. Although their knowledge of mathematics and science fields was clearly high school knowledge, it was not simply "shadow capital," which was predominantly the case among the Buffalo students. In other words, for these Denver students, their considerations were linked to some understanding of a range of academic fields of study as well as the careers themselves. It is hard to tell how well thought out these decisions were, or how deep the students' knowledge actually was, but they had some sense of what comprised a field of study. This is in sharp contrast to "shadow capital" in STEM that characterized much of what passed as high school knowledge in Buffalo. At the very least, for the students who could make these decisions, they brought a great sense of relief that a choice had been made!

EXPERIENCES IN COLLEGE

We were not able to continue our ethnographic work with the focal students once they left high school in 2013; thus, we do not have detailed information about their college experiences or their reasons for continuing in or leaving a STEM field during college. However, we did survey them once in 2015 and again in 2019, and we also conducted semi-structured interviews with some of them in 2019. During this period, we were able to contact thirty-seven (77 percent) of the forty-eight focal students from Denver who were original participants in our study. This information enabled us to identify STEM outcomes in terms of college major and education beyond college, as of 2019, for some of the students. This information appears in tables 7.1 and 7.2 of this chapter.

Again, it is striking to note that twenty-five (52 percent) of the forty-eight original Denver focal students continued into college in a STEM field in 2013. All but two of the twenty-five were still pursuing some form of STEM in 2015 after two years of college. By 2019, we were able to verify that nineteen (76 percent) of the twenty-five had graduated from either a two- or four-year college in a STEM field.

TRAJECTORIES OF IDENTIFICATION IN STEM

The forty-eight original focal students from Denver were all "high achievers" in math or science or both, based on ninth-grade standardized test scores. They (and their parents and teachers) agreed to participate in our study, and most of the focal students participated for nine years. But they did not attend high schools serving mostly privileged students, nor were they from economically privileged families themselves. We also over-sampled to increase racial/ethnic diversity among the focal students at each school. These are not the kinds of students who are generally expected to stand out in high school STEM, to pursue STEM into college, or to graduate with STEM degrees. Yet, 40 percent (nineteen) of the original group of forty-eight focal students in Denver accomplished this.

In this chapter, we have focused on how this group of students came to identify themselves in STEM over four years of high school. We found somewhat conflicting influences on their trajectories of identification in STEM. From the start, these students were known and labeled as "good students" in math or science, and, for the most part, they received high grades in these subjects to "prove" it. They were also placed in advanced or faster-tracked classes, ever more so as they proceeded through high school. Although their classes may not have been the most academically rigorous, especially at the STEM-focused schools (Chavez and Pella), they were the "top" on offer at each school. These conditions worked in concert to produce focal student identities as "really good" and "the best" in math or science.

At the same time, as we have shown in previous chapters, promised STEM opportunities in the Denver schools were somewhat eroded, although not nearly as seriously as in Buffalo. The figured worlds of STEM were "hollowed out," but were not as limiting as those in Buffalo. These findings hold even when Capital is removed from the analysis. This seems far from an ideal situation for developing strong identities in STEM, yet some of the students in Denver did just that, at least as evidenced in their STEM-related college and postcollege opportunities and choices.

Our data suggest that the Denver focal students, especially the girls, who succeeded in STEM through college found crucial support for continued identification in STEM from individuals or groups who provided it when it mattered most—in eleventh and twelfth grades when confidence in STEM was shaken by more advanced coursework that made it harder for students to meet their well-learned expectations of what it means to be "good" in math or science. Some of this support came because the students themselves sought it out, as when someone decided (perhaps for the first time) to ask a teacher for help after school. Some came when perceptive teachers reached out with extra help or encouragement and were willing to give it consistently. Some came from individuals outside of school whom focal students encountered when they attended low-cost or free-of-charge STEM-related camps, workshops, seminars, or college visits. And undoubtedly, some came from family and community members. These supports could not ensure that focal students would continue on a STEM trajectory, but we would argue that for the girls in our study, they were critical at a time during high school when the students' identification with STEM was especially vulnerable.[15] These supports did not seem similarly important for boys, a topic that deserves further research.

Our finding that some students were able to pursue STEM does not absolve the schools (or society) of responsibility for eroded opportunity structures or hollowed-out figured worlds, both of which comprise key topics in this volume. But it does suggest that early identification of self as "good in" math or science, as constructed in school, can be nurtured in ways that serve to broaden participation in STEM. In this regard, it is particularly striking that in only one of the schools (Capital) among the eight in our study did counseling staff give much attention to the students who were doing well in school; that is, the students were not in danger of flunking out, were not disruptive, and/or were not in crisis. And in no case was any special attention given (to our knowledge) to students with interests in or intentions to pursue STEM, even in ostensibly STEM-focused schools. Students like the focal students who are already "good" in math or science in high school, however defined, would seem to be especially good candidates to receive more attention and guidance in the effort to broaden participation and success in STEM.

The findings in this chapter make clear that some of the focal students in our study were able to overcome systemic constraints and move forward in STEM, and to do so in competitive universities and challenging STEM fields. Their commitment to being good students in high school math or science, their support networks, and their own initiative enabled them to remain interested in STEM, graduate from college in STEM, attend graduate and professional schools in STEM, and, in many cases, move into STEM-related work fields. As we see in chapter 6, this was much less the case in the schools studied in Buffalo than in those in Denver. Having said this, even in Denver, which, as we see throughout this volume, provided more sustained STEM-related opportunities than did Buffalo, focal students still had to manage this success in the face of a system that provided them fewer STEM opportunities than desired, little or no STEM-specific counseling, and less-than-exciting figured worlds of STEM. This system, intended to broaden STEM participation among underrepresented and marginalized students, was not sufficient to the task, leaving many STEM "high achievers" in Denver, and particularly in Buffalo, unable to reach their goals.

CHAPTER 8

Minding the Gaps

Researchers and others have long known that school opportunities, including opportunities for academic achievement and attainment, postsecondary entrance and graduation, and short- and long-term employment prospects and income, are linked in ways that disadvantage low-income and minoritized students. Over the years, many different educational reforms have been proposed to disrupt this pattern.[1] In spite of these efforts and the notable expansion of the US system of education during the twentieth century, educational inequalities have persisted.[2] About this, Jaekyung Lee writes, "Currently, the United States is at war, and the nation's future is at risk. The war to which I refer is the war on student achievement gaps, a war that began decades ago and has proved extremely difficult to fight and complex to understand."[3]

STEM REFORM AS A SYSTEM

STEM education reform—the nationwide push to increase learning, achievement, and participation in science, technology, engineering, and mathematics—has a prominent present-day role in this war against achievement and attainment gaps. Schools have been central to this STEM reform effort and are being challenged to use more "systemic" approaches both to designing learning environments that advance coherent understandings of STEM and to attracting and encouraging more and different students to pursue STEM.[4] "Inclusive STEM-focused" public high schools and STEM curricular enhancements at public comprehensive high schools have been promoted as a means of pursuing these goals. In contrast to other recent reform efforts that concentrate on improving standardized testing and replacing teachers and principals when students' scores do not improve, inclusive STEM schools and STEM curricular enhancements are a particularly hopeful version of reform. This particular reform movement centers change on improving STEM curricula, incorporating technological advances, and specifically in the case of inclusive STEM public schools, increasing STEM-related educational and occupational prospects for lower-income and underrepresented minoritized students. Within this historical context, we embarked on our three-year in-school ethnographic study and subsequent longitudinal follow-up of practices and outcomes related to STEM school reform efforts in eight schools in two large US cities, Denver, Colorado, and Buffalo, New York.

The four high schools we studied in each city were generally representative of large-city schools in the United States. However, they served a higher proportion of low-income students (as indicated by free and reduced lunch [FRL] rates) and minoritized students, largely Black and Latino/a, than many schools in large-city districts (see the appendix for details). This is important in terms of potential generalizability of our findings to similarly situated schools and cities in the United States. Additionally, as we noted earlier in this volume, unlike in some places where state officials have directed and monitored STEM reform, the efforts in Denver and Buffalo were initiated and developed primarily in local districts by administrators, school leaders, and community members.[5] We do not claim generalizability beyond institutions such as those in our sample.

Also important to note, the ninety-six focal students (roughly twelve from each school) we attempted to follow closely from grade 10 to grade 12 and then into and beyond college (2010–2019) were originally selected *because* they attended non-privileged high schools, *because* they were in the top 20 percent of the high school class based on their grade 9 standardized achievement scores in math and science, and *because* they indicated an interest in pursuing one or more STEM fields when they entered grade 10. Within this group, we over-sampled for minoritized students who agreed to participate. As it turned out, we were able to follow sixty-three of the original ninety-six (66 percent) focal students over the nine-year period of our study, giving us the rare ability to document in detail the high school to college to work trajectories of precisely the kind of students for whom current STEM reforms and subsequent prospective employment are intended. The ability to connect STEM opportunities and experiences directly with specific diverse student outcomes is the special strength of our work.

Overall in this volume, we show that in neither city did the enthusiasm and intention to reform STEM education fully translate into meaningful or sustained improvements. *Good intentions were not enough.* Newly formed career academies focused on STEM fields could not be sustained in the Denver schools, and overall high hopes and good intentions quickly collided with state-level graduation requirements and accountability demands there. These "mechanisms of erosion" were particularly evident in Buffalo, where few traces of promised and initially enhanced opportunities for STEM remained over the course of our three-year ethnographic investigation in the schools. Furthermore, STEM capital actually offered and produced in the Buffalo schools often comprised "shadow capital"—a form of capital that "outwardly resembles yet contains only traces of dominant cultural capital, thus failing to yield the same kind of exchange value in the postsecondary marketplace."[6] Relative to Denver, such "shadow capital" was not a commodity that the Buffalo students could reliably utilize for entry into four-year competitive colleges, a range of STEM majors, lucrative STEM jobs, or social mobility.

We further show that college and career counseling opportunities for high-achieving students interested in STEM were woefully inadequate in the schools in both cities. School guidance counselors were inundated with tasks related to accountability mandates (attendance rates, dropout rates, graduation rates, etc.) and with students in crisis. They had little if any time to devote to students who were doing well in high school—defined by guidance counselors as "on track to graduate"—and they were not, in most cases, prepared to provide guidance in support of students' expanding interests in STEM fields. Again, the situation was somewhat better (though not ideal) in Denver, where school personnel established partnerships with local colleges and nonprofit organizations to provide some college counseling and career support. This kind of counseling support was not available in the Buffalo schools.

Finally, we show that interpretive schemes or "figured worlds" that circulated in the Denver and Buffalo schools we studied were "hollowed out" in ways that limited development of STEM knowledge and skills. These figured worlds assigned meaning, value, and prestige to those who did "well" in math or science by simply following instructions and making good grades in Denver and simply "passing" in Buffalo. Although the figured world of being "good in" math or science in Denver left much to be desired, it contributed more to the development of STEM identities among a notable number of girls in particular in our Denver sample, than the figured world of "passing" did for *any* of the students in our Buffalo sample.

The stark reality of far fewer advanced math and science courses, fewer opportunities for college counseling, the predominance of "shadow STEM capital," and the figured world of "passing" in the Buffalo schools markedly constrained short- and long-term postsecondary opportunities for college and STEM compared to students in Denver. Denver students were able to complete notably more high-level advanced math and science courses (here defined as IB or AP) than was the case for Buffalo. Denver students had far greater success in gaining entrance to more competitive undergraduate postsecondary institutions, particularly in STEM; earning undergraduate STEM degrees from more competitive postsecondary institutions; continuing to pursue STEM in graduate and professional school, at times at very prestigious institutions; and pursuing STEM careers. Taking nothing away from the hard work of the Buffalo students who held onto a vision of pursuing STEM throughout high school, outcome data make clear that the STEM-related trajectories of the students in the two cities, when largely controlling for demographic characteristics, were markedly different.

THEORETICAL IMPLICATIONS

Accumulating Consequences

Theories of cumulative (dis)advantage posit a situation in which individuals, groups, or institutions that are initially the same or highly similar diverge over time as advantages accumulate for some while disadvantages accumulate for others. In our case, as described in chapter 1, the schools in Denver and Buffalo were similar in that they were non-criterion, large-city public high schools that served large percentages of low-income and minoritized students. They were also similar in confronting and embracing the need for STEM education reform. The focal students from the eight schools were relatively similar in that they were all designated "high achieving" in math and science, and they were all interested in pursuing STEM when our study began. The striking gap in STEM outcomes between the focal students in the two cities (even when Capital is omitted) led us to consider the applicability of cumulative (dis)advantage theories to our work.

Writing about the theory of cumulative advantage (CA), Thomas DiPrete and Gregory Eirich summarize the central idea as follows:

[T]he advantage of one individual or group over another grows (i.e., accumulates) over time, which is often taken to mean that the inequality of this advantage grows over time. The advantage in question is typically a key resource or reward in the stratification process, for example, cognitive development, career position, income, wealth, or health . . . [Thus, cumulative advantage] becomes part of an explanation for growing inequality when current levels of accumulation have a direct causal relationship on future levels of accumulation. A CA process is capable of magnifying small differences over time and makes it difficult for an individual or group that is behind at a point in time in educational development, income, or other measures to catch up. Ironically, despite the obvious theoretical and policy importance of CA models, and despite widespread references to their existence in the literature, the sustained development and testing of CA models has been more the exception than the rule.[7]

More recently, Michelle Maroto has discussed the importance of accumulating *disadvantage*. Focusing on bankruptcy, she argues that "in the case of bankruptcy, financial hardship unfolds over a specific series of events, which can lead to the accumulation of disadvantage connected to changes in employment, marital, and health status." She notes: "The effects of job loss on bankruptcy become more apparent as these events accumulate over time, and limit wealth creation . . . As a whole, my findings demonstrate how adverse events and financial hardship lead to bankruptcy [i.e., accumulated disadvantage] through multiple pathways."[8] In the context we studied, accumulating disadvantages in the Buffalo schools (compared to those in Denver) led to a particular version of what might be considered *"educational* bankruptcy," with short- and long-term consequences for the very students who were the target of the STEM school reform. By this, we do not mean to imply that the Buffalo students did not receive any education, as this is not the case. However, they accumulated disadvantages, over time, that limited rather than expanded their future opportunities relative to comparably capitalized students in Denver. As we see clearly in chapters 6 and 7, Denver students across all four sampled institutions continued to accumulate advantages that worked to substantially expand their opportunities moving forward relative to students in Buffalo.

This type of cumulative advantage or disadvantage, developing through multiple pathways over time in our study, highlights the power and potential of schools *to boost or constrain* developing inequality. Initially comparable reform efforts took hold over time in each city in such a way as *to compound, rather than disrupt or alter,* any early entering differences between the schools and students in our study. As entering differences were relatively small, the compounding of cumulative adverse effects related to more limited STEM course offerings and college and STEM counseling in Buffalo, the presence of shadow STEM capital, and the figured world of "passing" *increased the gap, over time,* between Buffalo focal students and those in Denver, further disadvantaging those in Buffalo.

As anticipated by theories of cumulative (dis)advantage, differences became larger over time, and it became harder and harder for those "left behind" to make up any relative loss. We see the extent to which differences become larger over time most clearly in the outcome data reported in chapters 6 and 7, when entering postsecondary students from Buffalo were at a markedly increased disadvantage relative to their Denver peers and relative to their own disadvantage in relation to Denver when entering grade 10. By the time the Buffalo students were considering graduate and professional school, the Denver students had notably stronger dossiers for admission. By the time the Denver students were applying for STEM jobs, they had even stronger dossiers for consideration as compared to students from Buffalo. Without serious attempts to equalize the playing field in high school, relatively small initial disadvantages can become insurmountable after years of accumulating disadvantages.

Effectively Maintained Inequality

Our findings also bear on what Samuel Lucas calls "effectively maintained inequality."[9] At a general level, effectively maintained inequality recognizes that educational expansion at any given level is often accompanied by increasing institutional differentiation or heightened internal systemic stratification. While STEM education expansion is certainly desirable and well intended, the unrealized promise of STEM education reform in Buffalo put these low-income and minoritized students further behind, not only *relative to those with privilege, but relative to those of comparable demographic characteristics who attended schools such as those in Denver.* While Denver did not fully meet the promises embedded in its own STEM education reform effort, the Denver students continued to accumulate advantages, in and beyond high school and in and beyond the postsecondary sector, a point made abundantly clear in chapters 6 and 7. In contrast, the comparable student population in Buffalo continued to accumulate disadvantages over time, thereby increasing institutional differentiation between schools that served largely comparable populations and heightening systemic stratification. While an *individual* student can perhaps recoup from accumulated disadvantage over the long run, the group cannot follow. Our study highlights the collective mechanisms through which relatively small inequalities accumulate and compound during high school and are then subsequently carried into the postsecondary and occupational sectors, where they become increasingly larger over time, substantially exacerbating inequality.

METHODOLOGICAL STRENGTHS

Education researchers have long called for studies that focus on linkages between precollege experiences, postsecondary entrance and completion patterns, and field of study.[10] This so-called "pipeline" has usually been investigated quantitatively. Virtually no one has taken a multisited ethnographic longitudinal approach, including both qualitative and descriptive quantitative data collection and analysis, to tracking specific groups of students, over time, from high school through postsecondary entrance, field of study, college graduation, and location in the occupational sector. In fact, few ethnographic longitudinal investigations have been conducted at all, rendering our study distinctive. The strength of our approach enabled us to investigate and contextualize available moves and choices made by low-income and minoritized actors as they encountered STEM opportunity structures and interpretive schema from sophomore year in high school into and through postsecondary destinations, including, in the case of Denver, graduate and professional school.

WHERE TO GO FROM HERE: LESSONS LEARNED

Urban STEM education reform is a laudable and ambitious project for schools and society. It has been envisioned as contributing to a "new city" in which millions of young people are prepared for a brighter future.[11] *But good intentions are not enough.* As our findings reveal, it will take vision, planning, commitment, continued monitoring, hard work, resources, and time. We are asking a lot of the school system, individual schools, people who work in or for them, and students who attend them.

To begin with, our findings make clear that we need coherent, sustained, and advanced STEM course offerings for students who are interested in pursuing STEM in college and who score well in math and science proficiency tests relative to their schools in grade 9. In addition, when students falter and are unable to proceed to the next higher math and science course in a predictable and sustained sequence of STEM course offerings, we must consider offering STEM "booster shots," a se-

ries of intense encounters with course content that students are struggling with.[12] This could be done throughout the year, but also during
the summers in a series of "boot camps" for high-achieving students
from low-income families who are interested in pursuing STEM. Such
boot camps could be funded by agencies such as the National Science
Foundation, the Institute of Education Sciences, and similarly minded
private foundations desiring increased opportunities for low-income
and underrepresented minoritized students.[13] Rigorous research must
accompany these interventions, with an eye to adjusting "boot camp
formulas" under specific conditions and with varying populations of
students. Students in private and public schools that serve privileged
students offer such "booster shots" routinely, as they "pile up" high-
level experiences specifically as related to STEM.[14] It is time we offer
such advantages to talented low-income and minoritized students who
wish to pursue STEM in college and career.

Additionally, we need dedicated guidance counseling for college and
STEM careers in all their variety and for all students. We need figured
worlds that make it a badge of honor to be "good in" school math or science in all its richness and complexity. Such needs can also be addressed
in boot camps for low-income and minoritized students. We also need
the ability to develop supportive articulations between STEM education
reform and high school graduation requirements, federal and state accountability demands, and other mandates and programs. We cannot
expect, nor would we want, STEM education to be the only thing that
schools do; thus, we must find ways to develop not only strong STEM
education programs but also productive articulations among all the
needs and demands related to making schools better.

In Denver, we see steps in the right direction with notable expan-
sions of STEM offerings, including more courses and more advanced
courses. Importantly, in Denver, such courses were offered in a se-
quenced manner so as to scaffold success at the next level. In other
words, these additions were supported by programs that allowed and
encouraged students to *move coherently and successfully* through course
sequences culminating in Precalculus or Calculus in math and Chemistry and Physics in science. Unlike Buffalo, they were also supported

by opportunities for students to take accelerated math in grade 9; the absence of hard borders to progression through courses such as the Regents examination system in New York State; and the availability of enough students to sufficiently enroll in higher-level and advanced courses—thereby making them consistently available. And, to a greater extent than in Buffalo, they were also supported by external partnerships that delivered some college and career counseling when in-school guidance counselors were diverted to other tasks.

Also in Denver, we see constraints and limits on these positive steps. We see that enrollment numbers for advanced courses could still be too low to offer the courses. We see that neither school personnel nor parents demanded that ways be found to provide these courses; and we see that the college and career counseling that was offered did not meet the demand for it nor did it focus specifically on support for students interested in pursuing a STEM field. Again, we strongly recommend that these issues be addressed in boot camps for promising students drawn from nonselective, non-charter public schools, wherein those at the top of their respective classes in their schools (such as our focal students) have the opportunity to gain sustained advantage during organized after-school and weekend encounters, as well as summers. The fact is that the vast majority of low-income and underrepresented minoritized students in the United States attend schools such as our sampled institutions, and this is not likely to change, given their numbers and the realities of their living situations. It is time to intentionally focus on improving opportunities *within* the kinds of schools that the vast majority of low-income and underrepresented minoritized students attend in this country. There will never be enough alternative institutions to absorb the pool of talented students in STEM who currently attend non-criterion, non-charter institutions such as those in our study. Rather than focusing solely on special schools for talented students, we need to enhance conditions and opportunities in STEM in those schools more widely attended by students such as our focal students.

About ten years ago, we presented the first of many papers about this study at the annual meeting of the American Educational Research

Association. Early in our work, we realized that STEM education reform efforts, especially in Buffalo, had stalled in the study schools and that the focal students' math and science experiences were already being compromised. One respondent to our paper, Dr. Na'ilah Suad Nasir, now president of the Spencer Foundation, posed the following question: "For whom is this acceptable?" More concretely, she asked, "In what contexts and for whom is this allowed to continue"? It is most certainly the case that if the production of disadvantage relative to other communities was taking root in wealthier communities, families who send their children to the schools would not stand for it. More economically capitalized parents would exercise their option to transfer their children, one way or another, to other institutions—whether private or public; school bonds would be voted down; and administrators would likely lose their jobs, if the situation was not rectified in a timely manner. Parents in privileged communities fight hard for the right of their children to have first-rate opportunities available in schools while being conscious of the fact that first-rate opportunities are never fully equally distributed. Having said this, there is a floor beneath which lack of opportunities would not be tolerated by parents or the community at large.

Privileged parents feel it is their right and even their duty to contest woefully inadequate educational opportunities for their own children, and they do so with great alacrity. If opportunities are not strengthened, these parents "vote with their feet" and simply exit the school, as they have the resources to do so. *While less privileged parents feel exactly the same way in that they desperately want their schools to work for their children*, the sad point is that the schools often do not do so. This makes the work of the schools and school personnel that serve less highly capitalized communities that much more important.

A particularly sad fact is that the Buffalo students in our study believed in themselves and kept moving forward in spite of processes of cumulative disadvantage that defined their schooling experience relative to Denver students, and, even more clearly, relative to more highly capitalized students who attended schools that took the job of authentic education more seriously over time. Although the schools seemed to give up on the Buffalo students, the Buffalo students never gave up on themselves. Coming from modest backgrounds, they nevertheless tried to keep moving forward. While many Denver students gained cumulative advantages and ultimately capitalized on these advantages, the Buffalo students, to their credit, did not give up. We owe these smart and dedicated students much more than we gave them.

Studies that shine a spotlight on what went right and what went wrong in what began as a genuine effort to broaden opportunities for low-income and minoritized students in two US cities are critically important. We must take a systemic approach to learning from the failings of this effort while capitalizing on its successes.

Our study reveals that general enthusiasm and promising proposals for STEM education reform exist, but these starting points need more support than they are getting, especially in schools serving low-income and minoritized students. At the high school level, enthusiasm and innovative proposals must be backed up with solid, sequential, and consistent STEM curricula; they must be backed up with counseling that focuses on supporting STEM interests and STEM prospects; they must be backed up with interpretive models in high schools that prioritize values and achievements of authentic (rather than bureaucratic) mathematics and science. This can profitably happen in "STEM boot camps" that provide a *rigorous* set of afterschool and summer experiences to talented students to make them competitive for college and career in STEM. Such camps could be staffed by some of the most talented teachers in the nation who wish to participate, with an eye to opportunities specifically tailored to talented low-income and minoritized students interested in math and science. These camps would need to be subject to the same kind of rigorous research that characterizes research in other fields so as to continually monitor and improve processes and outcomes. Grants could be awarded based on competitive proposals subject to rigorous review.

Goals such as these cannot be achieved by individual schools on their own, yet they are not insurmountable. Other possibilities also exist: ways to group together high-achieving students from several schools to offer an array of advanced STEM (and other) courses could be arranged; external partnerships that facilitate college and career counseling like those in Denver could be expanded and mentors with STEM experiences included; symbolic resources that highlight rewards and prestige for excellence (rather than conformity and "passing") in STEM courses, interests, and activities could be developed; and accountability indicators could include success in preparing high school students for STEM in college and beyond.

POSTSCRIPT

We want to be very clear that our intent in writing this book is to show how a major educational reform initiative was taken up in eight non-privileged high schools serving mostly low-income and minoritized students in two representative cities from 2010 to 2019. The fact that we found accumulating differences and uneven outcomes should not be taken as a wholesale criticism of STEM education reform efforts. We know, for example, that some researchers, including Barbara Means and Sharon Lynch, have found positive outcomes associated with inclusive STEM-focused schools and other STEM reform initiatives.[15] We ourselves found some positive outcomes, especially in Denver, despite systemic limitations. Even in Buffalo, where there were more limitations and fewer counteractions, some of the students did relatively well— completing college and obtaining good jobs.[16]

Our findings also should not be taken as criticism of the specific districts, schools, or individuals involved; many worked hard every day to make the best of challenging situations. What *must* be criticized are the workings of the educational system as a whole, whereby initiatives that are well conceived and well intentioned alone serve to confuse, contradict, or undermine each other when they must work in relation to each other in practice and over time. In our case, STEM reform initiatives, curricular needs, accountability demands, shadow capital, and hollowed-out interpretive schema worked together, sometimes in supportive but often in non-reinforcing or even conflicting ways. What we found about STEM reform initiatives could be the case in any large US city that serves comparable students in its public high schools, but it need not be. We cannot continue to let our top math and science underrepresented minoritized students fall behind more privileged students in STEM. America can do better, and it is time that we do so in the kinds of nonselective large-city high schools that the vast majority of such students attend. More than ever, we must "mind the gaps." Anything less will result in our continuing to lose generations of talented students who could contribute in multiple important and stunning ways in STEM.

Research Methodology

This study is composed of two interrelated parts. In Part I, we undertook a three-year (2010–2013) comparative and longitudinal ethnographic study of STEM-related opportunities in eight inclusive urban public high schools in Denver, Colorado, and Buffalo, New York. Four of the high schools were urban comprehensive (traditionally organized) schools, and four identified as intentionally STEM focused in some way. In Part II, we conducted a four-year follow-up study (2015–2019) of the original focal students. Here we outline the methods used in each major component. Additionally, we discuss the representativeness of the schools and students sampled in our study.

PART I: THREE-YEAR SCHOOL-BASED ETHNOGRAPHIC INVESTIGATION

School Site Selection

In both cities, the majority of all students (> 92 percent) attended public, neighborhood, non-charter schools.[1] Selection of schools for our study was dependent on (1) designation as a STEM-focused or traditional high school by each local district; (2) evidence of a high percentage of low-income and minoritized students; and (3) willingness on the part of the school to participate in the study and, in the case of Buffalo, recommendation of the Superintendent of Schools. In Denver, researchers constructed a list of prospective schools (based on demographics and school type) and requested permission from individual school principals. From our original list, one comprehensive school declined to participate, and we substituted another (Capital) which was not as comparable a site as we had originally hoped for.

The four schools selected in Denver were in three adjacent urban school districts. Capital and Southside (all school names are pseudonyms) were large comprehensive high schools in the same district; each had maintained a traditional structure for many years. Chavez and Pella were comprehensive high schools until recently when both were reorganized into career academy schools.[2] In 2010 when the study began, Chavez had five academies, one of which was STEM focused: the Engineering Academy. Pella also had five academies, two of which were STEM focused: the Engineering Academy and the Health/Medicine Academy.

In Buffalo, all four schools were part of the same urban school district. Two schools, Broadway Science and Lincoln, were comprehensive high schools, while Global Horizons and STEM Academy were small schools, developed in line with the tenets of the small schools movement and intended to focus on STEM. In Buffalo, we began the school selection process by asking the Superintendent of Schools to provide the names of public, non-criterion, non-charter high schools that met our selection criteria (serving a high proportion of low-income and minoritized students and having either a traditional or a STEM focus). His suggested list of school sites mirrored the list assembled by our own research team in conversation with one of our Advisory Board members—a SUNY Distinguished Professor of Chemistry—who similarly had ongoing projects in the district. We worked to match relevant student and school characteristics within and across cities as much as possible.

After selecting and receiving permission from the eight targeted schools, the principal investigators met with school administrators, teachers, and counselors to provide details about the study and enlist participation. Data were then drawn from district and school documents; interviews that were conducted with math and science teachers, counselors, and focal students at each school; and observations that were made in designated classrooms and school common areas. Consistent with our research questions, interviews with students, teachers, and counselors focused on their experiences and responses to STEM-related opportunities at their respective institutions. School documents included published ninth- through twelfth-grade course offerings, sequences, prerequisites, academies, and tracks. In addition, official student transcripts provided data on actual courses taken, grades received, and, in some cases, standardized test scores.

Data Collection at Each School

Senior researchers were primarily responsible for obtaining access to the district and the schools and developing and maintaining relationships with school and district staff. Junior researchers (postdoctoral researchers and graduate students) developed close relationships with focal students, their families, and school staff through regular interviews and visits during the course of the study.

At least one principal, one science teacher, and one math teacher were interviewed each year in each school. Principals were asked to discuss their background, the history of the school and its student composition, and any programs for or commitments to STEM education and reform. Teachers were asked to discuss their background, the school, their students, parents, and existing school-based preparation for STEM in college and career. Sample questions included, among others: In what ways does this school emphasize STEM fields? Are there any special programs in place to encourage students at this school to go to college in STEM fields? What do you think will affect the likelihood of students' success in STEM?

At least one counselor with responsibility for students in grades 10 through 12 was interviewed at each school site each year. Counselors were asked to discuss counseling activities, course planning and selection, college admissions, and STEM opportunities. Questions included, among others: How do you decide which math and science classes to offer, and how do you assign students to math and science classes? Are there any special programs in place to encourage students to go to college? Are there any special programs in place to encourage students to pursue STEM? What do you think will affect the likelihood of students' success in STEM fields?

At least twelve focal students from among tenth graders at each school were purposefully selected for in-depth interviews. Focal students were invited to participate based on the following criteria: (1) tenth-grade standing in the 2010–11 academic year (the 2009–10 high school cohort); (2) ranked in the top 20 percent of their high school class in math and science (as determined by math and science grades, state standardized test scores in math and science, and counselor and teacher affirmation); and (3) a stated interest (at the time) in pursuing STEM-related studies at the postsecondary level. We chose high achievers in math and science because they seemed the most likely to participate in the high-level STEM opportunities offered by the high schools and the most likely to be prepared for postsecondary STEM. Thus, our claims about students' opportunities and outcomes in this book were intentionally limited to a select group of high achievers (relative to their school), and their experiences at each school.

To select the focal student sample and with permission from each school, we initially assembled a list of all students in the top 20 percent of the class in math and science based on the above criteria. For those who expressed interest in participating in our study, we verbally assessed potential interest in STEM. We then approached qualifying students, described the study, and invited them to participate. If they accepted, we shared Institutional Review Board—approved informational materials, including consent forms, with them and asked them to go over the forms with their parents or guardians and to return the signed documents to us. The final sample consisted of twelve students at each school ($n = 96$ students in total) who were among the most proficient in STEM subjects relative to the remaining 80 percent at their school, who agreed to participate in the study, and who met all the consenting criteria.

Focal students were interviewed twice per year in each year of the three-year ethnographic investigation. Sample questions included, among others: What can you tell me about your math and science courses? How were you placed in these courses? How are you doing in these classes? Are you interested in anything STEM related for a career? Why/why not? We also conducted participant observation in math and science classrooms that included focal students, in guidance counseling suites or centers, in school common areas, and on school field trips. We intended to interview one parent or guardian of all focal students, asking questions about their knowledge of their child's math and science courses and future plans, but we were only able to arrange these interviews with a handful of parents at each school. This is not uncommon in studies of low-income populations, where contact information is unreliable and scheduling can be challenging.[3]

REPRESENTATIVENESS OF SAMPLED SCHOOLS
AND STUDENT POPULATIONS

In 2013, there were 13,873 large-city school districts in the United States, according to the National Center for Education Statistics (NCES).[4] Both Denver and Buffalo were classified as large cities, defined as "a central city of a consolidated metropolitan statistical area (CMSA) or MSA, with the city having a population greater than or equal to 250,000."[5] A large-city school district is defined as having 15,000 or more students.[6] Table A.1 compares the demographic characteristics of Denver and Buffalo school districts with large-sized districts in the United States.

Based on these data, we can see that Denver and Buffalo school districts, overall, served higher percentages of disadvantaged students than schools in the large-city category, with an average of 72 percent of students receiving free or reduced lunch (FRL) in Denver and 79 percent in Buffalo, compared to only 52 percent of students in comparable schools across the US. Buffalo had substantially higher percentages

TABLE A.1 *Comparison of the demographic characteristics of Denver and Buffalo school districts with US schools in large-sized urban areas, 2013*[a]

	DENVER	BUFFALO	US SCHOOLS IN LARGE CITIES
District size: Large city	86,046	34,854	
% free or reduced lunch	72.0	79.0[b]	52.0
% White	21.2	21.4	20.7
% African American	13.8	50.1	26.5
% Hispanic	57.7	17.4	41.4
% Asian American	3.3	7.3	7.6

[a]Data are found in Thomas D. Snyder, Christobal De Brey, and Sally A. Dillow, "Digest of Education Statistics 2015, NCES 2016-014," *National Center for Education Statistics* (2016), https://nces-ed-gov.gate.lib.buffalo.edu/pubs2016/2016014.pdf.

[b]This figure is taken from 2011 data, not 2013 data, due to unavailability of complete data for 2013. Data are found in Thomas D. Snyder, Christobal De Brey, and Sally A. Dillow, "Digest of Education Statistics 2015, NCES 2016-014," *National Center for Education Statistics* (2016), https://nces-ed-gov.gate.lib.buffalo.edu/pubs2016/2016014.pdf.

of Black students, similar percentages of White and Asian American students, and lower percentages of Hispanic students than schools in the comparison large-city-school national population. Denver has substantially higher percentages of Hispanic students, similar percentages of White students, and lower percentages of Asian American and Black students than schools in the comparison large-city school population.

Table A.2 shows the demographic characteristics of our eight schools in Denver and Buffalo compared to schools across the United States in large-sized city areas.

All eight schools in our sample have FRL percentages well over the US average of 52 percent, with a range from 64 percent (Capital) to 93 percent (Southside), with a mean of 78 percent. All are well above the percentage (52 percent) in the category used for purposes of comparison—US schools in large cities. Compared to the other schools in our study, Capital had a somewhat more highly capitalized population of students, although still above the national average for FRL in large-city districts.

Thus, although our sampled cities and institutions were generally representative of those in the large-city school category, as per NCES, our schools in both cities served a more concentrated population of both minoritized students and students who qualify for FRL than the overall average of schools represented in the comparison category. This is important in terms of potential generalizability of our findings to similarly situated schools and cities in the United States.

Data Analysis

For the site-based ethnographic portion of the study, data from school documents were organized in order to create a display of STEM-related courses officially available at each of the eight schools at the beginning of our study (2010). The course displays were compared to reports of course offerings, changes, or course cancellations in our interviews or observations with students and teachers; they were also compared to official student transcripts.

Interview and observational data were transcribed and entered into a qualitative data analysis program (ATLAS.ti, version 5.2 in Denver;

TABLE A.2 *Comparison of the demographic characteristics of Denver and Buffalo schools with US schools in large-sized urban areas, 2013*

	DENVER				BUFFALO				US SCHOOLS IN LARGE CITIES
	Chavez	Pella	Southside	Capital	Broadway Science Academy	STEM Academy	Global Horizons	Lincoln	
% Free or reduced lunch	74.0	74.0	93.0	64.0	77.0	80.0	86.0	77.0	52.0
Race/ethnicity*									
% White	14.0	24.1	3.2	44.1	3.0	9.0	10.0	7.0	20.7
% African American	3.4	2.1	1.0	17.5	94.0	84.0	55.0	87.0	26.5
% Hispanic	81.0	64.7	91.7	21.5	2.0	6.0	25.0	4.0	41.4
% Asian American	0.4	7.3	2.9	2.1	0.0	1.0	8.0	1.0	7.6

*Here we use the race/ethnicity categories as they appear in publications and data sets from the National Center for Education Statistics.

HyperRESEARCH, version 4.5 in Buffalo). These data were initially coded deductively using codes consistent with the definitions of opportunity structures and figured worlds that framed the study; these codes included course offerings, requirements, and views of school, STEM, self, and future plans, among others.[7] As coding proceeded, initially large coding categories were divided inductively (using codes originating in the data) into subcategories, and new inductive codes were added. Data segments were double and sometimes triple coded, as relevant, and consolidated under a set of subcodes (e.g., future plans, math courses, science courses, counseling, extracurricular activities, and online activities, among others) for each school and relevant group (e.g., teacher, student, counselor).

Once data from Years 1–3 were initially coded by one member of the research team, the coding was reviewed by at least one other researcher on the team, and discrepancies were discussed and discrete passages noted as exemplars of emerging themes. Major themes were validated by the diversity of team members' perspectives, colleagues' reviews of themes and associated data, and member checks with selected participants to clarify comments and intentions. Researchers in each city analyzed the data from the schools in their respective cities and conducted cross-site comparisons of their four schools. Cross-city site comparisons were conducted subsequently. To organize the data presented in this book, we selected telling quotes and passages from interviews and observations to illustrate the main topics and themes across the eight school sites.

PART II: FOUR-YEAR FOLLOW-UP STUDY OF FOCAL STUDENTS, 2015–2019

Outcome data about the post-high school experiences of the focal students were gathered as follows: (1) an online descriptive survey administered to all original focal students whom we were able to locate in 2015, two years after graduation from high school; and (2) face-to-face or remote Zoom/FaceTime/Skype interviews with as many of the original focal students as we could contact in 2017–2019.[8] We additionally analyzed end-of-high school individual student transcripts for as many of the original focal students as we could obtain. Further, we conducted online searches, based on existing social media connections—on Facebook, Twitter, and LinkedIn—to confirm and expand our knowledge of focal student outcomes.

To collect follow-up data, we followed best practices as designed by the National Science Foundation–funded Michigan State University team led by Dr. Barbara Schneider.[9] We first contacted students via *Select Survey*, a site that allowed us to collect survey information online. We notified them that we would be following up and encouraged them to respond when they heard from our research team. After notifying students, we followed up to get or confirm phone numbers. Then we contacted individual students personally.

Once our researchers heard from participants, they immediately moved to set up an interview time (and place, if applicable). Interviews occurred in quiet coffee shops, in libraries, or online. Researchers reported the highest response from participants contacted by text or phone. Facebook connections were next most effective. As we describe in chapter 6, despite our best efforts in both cities, we were more successful in reinterviewing Denver students than Buffalo students.

In total, we were able to contact and interview twenty-six of forty-eight Buffalo participants and thirty-seven of forty-eight Denver participants from 2015 through 2019. In Buffalo, we obtained follow-up data from six participants from STEM Academy, four participants from Lincoln, five participants from Broadway Science Academy, and eleven participants from Global Horizons. In Denver, we obtained follow-up data from eleven participants from Capital, nine participants from Chavez, ten participants from Pella, and seven participants from Southside. In the follow-ups, we asked students to reflect on the following:

- How has your interest in STEM areas changed since you attended [high school]?
- What college courses have you taken in STEM? Will you major in a STEM field? Why or why not?

- Do you consider yourself a good student? How do you measure your academic success?
- Do you feel you were ready/prepared for college? Why or why not?
- Are you working now? If so, doing what?
- When will you graduate and what is your plan beyond college?
- Where do you see yourself in ten years? What do you hope to accomplish in five or ten years?

This assemblage of data enabled us to track follow-up outcomes for a subset of our original focal students. These outcomes included patterns of advanced math and science course-taking in high school; enrollment in college; the extent to which students continued to pursue STEM in college; graduation from a four- or two-year institution; graduation with a STEM degree; and progress toward a further degree in STEM or a STEM career.

We followed data analysis procedures for the follow-up interview data similar to those employed for the school-based portion of the study. Simple percentages were additionally calculated with regard to post-high school outcomes from the data gathered in the follow-up descriptive surveys, follow-up interviews, and online searches. Further, using chi-square tests, we investigated whether the associations between location (Denver or Buffalo) and outcomes were statistically significant in our sample group. Results of chi-square tests reported in chapter 6 should be interpreted with caution as chi-square calculations are sensitive to sample size. Our analytic sample size ranges from eighteen to sixty-three, depending on the outcomes.

CAUTIONS REGARDING OUR FINDINGS

Of course, as with any study, there were limits to what we could do and what we could account for. Several features of our sample suggest some caution with respect to our findings. One of these was the difference in size between the Denver and Buffalo schools. Although we tried to match school and student demographic characteristics across the two cities, our final sample consisted of four large high schools (more than 1,000 students) in Denver and four smaller schools (between 250 and 1,000 students) in Buffalo. The smaller schools in Buffalo had a harder time offering an array of high-level STEM courses simply by virtue of their size, as the number of students available to take the courses was quite small. While small schools have many strengths, there are, nevertheless, fewer students who can be placed in any given high-level STEM course. As we show in chapter 3, lack of qualified or interested students contributed to high-level STEM course cancellations in Buffalo because there were not enough students to comprise a class.

Another difference between the Denver and Buffalo schools was the educational accountability regime in the two states. This difference also affected the availability of higher-level math and science courses in Buffalo. New York State required high school students to take at least one Regents-level (more difficult than a "regular" course but not as difficult as honors, AP, or IB courses) math and one Regents-level science course, pass these courses, and score a 65 or better on Regents examinations for the courses, in order to graduate from high school. As described in chapter 3, meeting this requirement was difficult for many Buffalo students, and many had to retake courses and Regents examinations in order to pass, thereby preventing them from moving on to higher-level courses. This situation further depressed the number of students available to fill higher-level courses. It is also arguably the case that the import of passing Regents exams contributed to the salience of "passing" in the figured world of school success in Buffalo. While the Regents structure is certainly well intended and largely well executed, it is also the case that the stringent Regents structure may be inadvertently contributing to accumulated disadvantage in the Buffalo context.

Colorado, in contrast, mandated proficiency tests in each subject area each year, and while the results were used by teachers to *inform* their work and by administrators to *evaluate* teacher performance, *they were not used to regulate student progress through course sequences or high school graduation.* Thus, the schools we studied in Denver were *doubly advantaged* (compared to Buffalo) in filling higher-level math and science courses by the greater number of students overall *and* the absence of an externally imposed hard barrier to advancement through course sequences.

Another potentially consequential feature of our sample is the fact that at the time our study began, seven of the eight sampled schools had recently undergone some form of "turnaround"; that is, they had been sanctioned for poor academic performance by the state and were required to meet certain achievement targets in order to stay open.[10] This designation is often associated with disruptions such as high teacher and principal turnover and hypervigilant attention to test scores and dropout rates. It has also led to the reorganization of failing schools into STEM schools, as happened at Chavez, Pella, STEM Academy, and Broadway Science before our study began. Although many large-city schools in the United States have faced or been threatened with turnarounds, this fact probably made STEM reform more difficult than it would have been in less vulnerable schools.

Another issue is a lack of equivalence between the Denver and Buffalo focal students with regard to math proficiency prior to grade 10. After our study began, we found that the tenth-grade focal students we had selected for our sample in Denver were more likely to have taken accelerated math courses in grade 9 (Geometry or above) than those in Buffalo (x^2 (2, $n = 63$) = 12.093, $p < .01$); see table A.3.

While it is true that taking accelerated math (in this case, Geometry or above) versus non-accelerated math courses in grade 9 suggests somewhat different math proficiency among incoming grade 9 students in the two cities, this initial placement pattern in and of itself does not explain the range of differential outcomes noted throughout this volume. In order for Denver students to be successful in advanced math courses throughout high school, two things had to be in place: (1) advanced courses had to be consistently available each year of high school, with a steady flow of students positioned to take them over four years; and (2) schools had to build on students' grade 9 incoming skills by scaffolding math content over four years in ways that enabled students to progress from lower- to higher-level courses. Denver did this and Buffalo did not. As a result, relatively modest differences between Denver and Buffalo in incoming math skills at the beginning of our study "compounded" over time in ways that led to the production of notable differences in math and science course-taking patterns in the two cities, with Buffalo students falling further and further behind every year. As we make clear in chapters 6 and 7, outcome data among comparably low-income and minoritized students show substantially *widening* outcomes, over time, among students in the two cities from grade 9 through undergraduate schools, graduate and professional schools, and the STEM occupational sector.

Finally, as we have already mentioned in chapter 6, we were not able to locate as many focal students from Buffalo once they left high school as we could in Denver. This difference limits the strength of the comparisons we can make regarding postsecondary outcomes for focal students in the two cities. As noted earlier, it is plausible that our data led us to *underestimate* the (negative) impact of STEM reform in Buffalo relative to that in Denver. Because the most successful focal students were, in all probability, most likely to respond to our interview or survey requests after completing high school, less successful focal students are likely underrepresented in the outcome data reported in chapter 6. Buffalo focal students who did not respond may have accumulated even greater disadvantage relative to Denver students than suggested by data reported in chapter 6.

TABLE A.3 *Relationship between city and accelerated ninth-grade math*

ACCELERATED IN NINTH GRADE		NO	YES	TOTAL	CHI-SQUARE*
Denver	n	12	25	37	
	%	37.50	62.50	100	
Buffalo	n	20	6	26	
	%	76.92	23.08	100	$p < .05$
Total	n	32	31	63	
	%	50.79	49.21	100	

Note: Ratios are presented by location. When the students took Geometry or above in math in ninth grade, they were classified as Accelerated in ninth grade.

*For the total sample, the results of the chi-square test show a significant relation between city location and accelerated ninth-grade math. The Denver students were positively associated with accelerated math coursework in ninth grade.

NOTES

CHAPTER 1

1. Erika C. Bullock, "Only STEM Can Save Us? Examining Race, Place, and STEM Education as Property," *Educational Studies* 53, no. 6 (2017): 628.

2. In this book, the term *Black* refers to students who come largely from intergenerational US-born Black families. In some cases, Black students in our study came from families that entered the country as recent immigrants or refugees. We use the term *Latino/a* to refer to people of Latin American descent currently living in the United States. When using published statistics or quoting from or referring to published works, we retain the racial/ethnic descriptors used in the original sources.

3. Catherine Riegle-Crumb, Barbara King, and Yasmiyn Irizarry, "Does STEM Stand Out? Examining Racial/Ethnic Gaps in Persistence Across Postsecondary Fields," *Educational Researcher* 48, no. 3 (2019): 133–44; Nancy Campos, "The Experiences of Black and Latinx Graduate Students in STEM: A Critical Race Perspective" (Order No. 28086988, 2020). Available from Dissertations & Theses @ SUNY Buffalo (2448645933), https://www-proquest-com.gate.lib.buffalo.edu/dissertations-theses/experiences-black-latinx-graduate-students-stem/docview/2448645933/se-2?accountid=14169.

4. Erin E. Peters-Burton et al., "Inclusive STEM High School Design: 10 Critical Components," *Theory into Practice* 53, no. 1 (2014): 64–71.

5. Grace Chen, "The Rising Popularity of STEM: A Crossroads in Public Education or a Passing Trend?," last modified November 11, 2019, https://www.publicschoolreview.com/blog/the-rising-popularity-of-stem-a-crossroads-in-public-education-or-a-passing-trend; Thomas Jerald and Corinne Williams, "The History of Specialized STEM Schools and the Formation and Role of the NCSSSMST," *Roeper Review* 32, no. 1 (2009): 17–24, https://doi.org/10.1080/02783190903386561.

6. Melanie LaForce et al., "Revisiting Race and Gender Differences in STEM: Can Inclusive STEM High Schools Reduce Gaps?," *European Journal of STEM Education* 4, no. 1 (2019): 8.

7. Martha Cecilia Bottia et al., "The Importance of Community Colleges in Students' Choice to Major in STEM," *Journal of Higher Education* 91, no. 7 (2020): 1116–48; Jennifer Gnagey and Stéphane Lavertu, "The Impact of Inclusive STEM High Schools on Student Achievement," *AERA Open* 2, no. 2 (2016): 1–21; Sandra L. Hanson, "STEM Degrees and Occupations Among Latinos: An Examination of Race/Ethnic and Gender Variation," *Race, Gender & Class* (2013): 214–31; LaForce et al., "Revisiting Race and Gender Differences in STEM"; Sharon J. Lynch, Erin Peters-Burton, and Michael Ford, "Building STEM Opportunities for All," *Educational Leadership* 72, no. 4 (2015): 54–60; Barbara Means et al., "Expanding STEM Opportunities Through Inclusive STEM-Focused High Schools," *Science Education* 101, no. 5 (2017): 681–715; Jonathan M. Vitale, Kevin Lai, and Marcia C. Linn, "Taking Advantage of Automated Assessment of Student-Constructed Graphs in Science," *Journal of Research in Science Teaching* 52, no. 10 (2015): 1426–50; Nimisha H. Patel, M. Suzanne Franco, and Larry G. Daniel, "Student Engagement and Achievement: A Comparison of STEM Schools, STEM Programs, and Non-STEM Settings," *Research in the Schools* 26, no. 1 (2019): 1–11; Guan Saw, "The Impact of Inclusive STEM High Schools on Student Outcomes: A Statewide Longitudinal Evaluation of Texas STEM Academies," *International Journal of Science and Mathematics Education* 17, no. 8 (2019): 1445–57; Colby Tofel-Grehl and Carolyn M. Callahan, "STEM High School Communities: Common and Differing Features," *Journal of Advanced Academics* 25, no. 3 (2014): 237–71; Matthew Wiswall et al., "Does Attending a STEM High School Improve Student Performance? Evidence from New York City," *Economics of Education Review* 40 (2014): 93–105.

8. We use the term *inclusive STEM-focused high schools* to encompass the variety and emerging nature of the current collection of high schools devoted, in some way, to STEM for underrepresented students.

9. By this we mean that among all students in the top 20% for math or science at each school, we chose as focal students those who were low-income and racial minorities whenever possible. Of course, we could only involve students (and their parents) who agreed to participate.

10. National Center for Women in Information Technology, *Computing Education and Future Jobs: A Look at National, State, and Congressional District Data* (Boulder, CO: National Center for Women in Technology, 2011).

11. Raj Chetty et al., "Where Is the Land of Opportunity? The Geography of Intergenerational Mobility in the United States," *The Quarterly Journal of Economics* 129, no. 4 (2014): 1553–623.

12. David Stern, Charles Dayton, and Marilyn Raby, "Career Academies: A Proven Strategy to Prepare High School Students for College and Careers," *Career Academy Support Network* (2010).
13. The Colorado statewide "open enrollment" system allows students to attend a school of their choice in any school district as long as the student or their parents/guardians provide the necessary transportation and the school of choice has space for additional students.
14. "School improvement plans" in Colorado require that each school district and each school create an annual plan for meeting its achievement and progress goals in line with state standards. Plans are approved by the state, and failure to meet designated goals in a designated period of time can result in school reorganization, sometimes called "school turnaround," or closure. A turnaround school has been generally defined by Mass Insight as "a dramatic and comprehensive intervention in a low-performing school that: a) produces significant gains in achievement within two years; and b) readies the school for the longer process of transformation into a high-performance organization" (Mass Insight, June 2010, *School Turnaround Models: Emerging Turnaround Strategies and Results*. Boston, MA: Mass Insight Education & Research Institute.)

    In Colorado, schools sanctioned for not meeting state standards have three years to show improvement. If they are not successful, they can be "turned around." Chavez was the only officially designated turnaround school in the Denver study group, but Pella and Southside had also been sanctioned for not meeting state standards and were operating under school improvement plans requiring substantial gains in achievement and college attendance.
15. As will be evident as our story of these schools continues, Capital was somewhat of an outlier from the start. It had a more racially balanced student population and a smaller percentage of students receiving free or reduced lunch than the other seven schools. In chapter 6, we discuss some implications of this difference.
16. Staff, "Dealing with Decline: Enrollment Losses in Buffalo Schools Are Educational, Management Challenge," *Buffalo News*, February 2, 2008, https://buffalonews.com/news/dealing-with-decline-enrollment-losses-in-buffalo-schools-are-educational-management-challenge/article_0475a2a1-a542-5870-a705-1c6a505940e9.html.
17. The first College Board schools opened in New York City in 2004, with the goal of providing low-income and underserved students with a rigorous college preparatory education. See https://web.archive.org/web/20110926075403; http://about.collegeboard.org/history.

18. The program name is a pseudonym.
19. Jeannie Oakes, "Investigating the Claims in *Williams v. State of California*: An Unconstitutional Denial of Education's Basic Tools?," *Teachers College Record* (2004): 1889–906.
20. As the numbers of focal students are small, however, these percentages must be interpreted with caution, as one additional student in any given racial/ethnic category can markedly alter percentage distributions.
21. https://ncses.nsf.gov/pubs/nsf21321/.

CHAPTER 2

1. Some sections of this chapter originally appeared in Margaret Eisenhart et al., "High School Opportunities for STEM: Comparing Inclusive STEM-Focused and Comprehensive High Schools in Two US Cities," *Journal of Research in Science Teaching* 52, no. 6 (2015): 763–89, https://doi.org/10.1002/tea.21213. Reproduced by permission.
2. We could not accurately determine changes at Pella due to a change in school boundaries and course titles during this period.
3. In Buffalo, comparable data were not available for 2006–2009 because New York State Regents course content changed (e.g., "integrated math" became "algebra" in 2009).
4. In New York State, Regents examinations are developed and administered by the New York State Education Department, under the authority of the Board of Regents. The Board of Regents in New York State oversees all public education, from preK to university. Regents exams, as they are colloquially known, are prepared by a coterie of teachers. They are mapped to learning standards for each course, field-tested, and evaluated before being administered. In order to graduate with an NYS Regents diploma, students must pass three Regents science classes and three Regents math classes, and must receive a grade of 65 or better on at least one Regents science exam and one Regents math exam.
5. Catherine Riegle-Crumb and Eric Grodsky, "Racial-Ethnic Differences at the Intersection of Math Course-Taking and Achievement," *Sociology of Education* 83, no. 3 (2010): 248–70, https://doi.org/10.1177/0038040710375689.
6. In most cases, Early College High School programs allow high school students to take a mix of high school and community college courses prior to high school graduation. Successful students earn a high school diploma and community college credits toward an associate's degree.
7. Grace Chen, "The Rising Popularity of STEM: A Crossroads in Public Education or a Passing Trend?," last modified November 11, 2019, https://

www.publicschoolreview.com/blog/the-rising-popularity-of-stem-a-cross roads-in-public-education-or-a-passing-trend; Thomas Jerald and Corinne Williams, "The History of Specialized STEM Schools and the Formation and Role of the NCSSSMST," *Roeper Review* 32, no. 1 (2009): 17–24, https://doi.org/10.1080/02783190903386561.

8. Sharon J. Lynch et al., "Understanding Inclusive STEM High Schools as Opportunity Structures for Underrepresented Students: Critical Components," *Journal of Research in Science Teaching*, 55 (2017): 712–48, http://doi.org/10.1002/tea.21437.

9. Lynch et al., "Understanding Inclusive STEM High Schools," 716.

10. This was the case at Southside in Denver. For more information about it, see Margaret Eisenhart et al., "High School Opportunities for STEM: Comparing Inclusive STEM-Focused and Comprehensive High Schools in Two US Cities," *Journal of Research in Science Teaching* 52, no. 6 (2015): 763–89, https://doi.org/10.1002/tea.21213.

CHAPTER 3

1. This quote is from a guidance counselor at STEM Academy in year three of our study, in which she indicates the erosion of courses that were likely to occur over the coming year due to falling enrollment numbers in certain classes.

2. Some sections of this chapter were originally published in Lois Weis et al., "In the Guise of STEM Education Reform: Opportunity Structures and Outcomes in the Inclusive STEM-Focused High Schools," *American Educational Research Journal* 52, no. 6 (2015): 1024–59. Reproduced by permission.

3. Staff, "Dealing with Decline: Enrollment Losses in Buffalo Schools Are Educational, Management Challenge," *Buffalo News*, February 2, 2008, https://buffalonews.com/news/dealing-with-decline-enrollment-losses-in -buffalo-schools-are-educational-management-challenge/article_0475a2a1 -a542-5870-a705-1c6a505940e9.html.

4. Unlike Denver, Advanced Placement offerings were the highest potential offerings in these particular Buffalo schools, as there were no International Baccalaureate courses available.

5. All proper names used in this book are pseudonyms.

6. Career and Technical Education (CTE) programs for high school students are intended to teach specific career skills that prepare students for immediate work opportunities, if desired.

7. Persistently lowest-achieving schools are defined as: (1) any Title I school in improvement, corrective action, or restructuring that (a) Is among the lowest-achieving five percent of Title I schools in improvement, corrective

action, or restructuring or the lowest-achieving five Title I schools in improvement, corrective action, or restructuring in a given state, whichever number of schools is greater; or (b) Is a high school that has had a graduation rate that is less than 60 percent over a number of years; and (2) any secondary school that is eligible for, but does not receive, Title I funds that (a) Is among the lowest-achieving five percent of secondary schools or the lowest-achieving five secondary schools in the State that are eligible for, but do not receive, Title I funds, whichever number of schools is greater; or (b) Is a high school that has had a graduation rate that is less than 60 percent over a number of years; and (3) to identify the lowest-achieving schools, a State must take into account both (i) The academic achievement of the "all students" group in a school in terms of proficiency on the State's assessments in reading/language arts and mathematics combined; and (ii) The school's lack of progress on those assessments over a number of years in the "all students" group. (As defined in the US Department of Education's Race to the Top District Competition draft, https://www.ed.gov/race-top/district-competition/definitions.)

8. It is important to note that the Forensics program was initially envisioned to be part of the science offerings rather than CTE, but this was changed without informing parents or students. By the time of our study, both Forensics and HOT were CTE. HOT was the last program to be added.

9. By way of clarification, course content in non-Regents courses is set locally; Regents course content is set by the New York State Board of Regents and culminates in a state-level examination. Regents courses are considered far more challenging than non-Regents courses by administrators, teachers, counselors, parents, and students. Admissions personnel in postsecondary institutions in the state of New York and elsewhere are aware of the difference between Regents and non-Regents courses, as well as Regents and AP courses.

10. Pierre Bourdieu, "The Forms of Capital," in *Handbook of Theory and Research for the Sociology of Education*, ed. John G. Richardson (New York: Greenwood Press, 1986); Pierre Bourdieu and Jean-Claude Passeron, *Reproduction in Education, Society, and Culture* (London: Sage Publications, 1977).

11. Douglas S. Massey, *Categorically Unequal: The American Stratification System* (New York: Russell Sage Foundation, 2007), 16.

12. For a related discussion of returns on college debt, see Rachel E. Dwyer, Randy Hodson, and Laura McCloud, "Gender, Debt, and Dropping Out of College," *Gender & Society* 27, no.1 (2013): 30–55.

13. William Julius Wilson, *The Truly Disadvantaged: The Inner City, the Underclass, and Public Policy* (Chicago: University of Chicago Press, 1987).

14. Kristin Cipollone and Amy E. Stich, "Shadow Capital: The Democratization of College Preparatory Education," *Sociology of Education* 90, no. 4 (2017): 333–54. Cipollone and Stich were postdoctoral researchers on our study, and data on shadow capital and figured worlds appeared in "Shadow Capital."

15. Kristin Cipollone, Amy E. Stich, and Lois Weis, "STEM for All: Student Identities and the Paradox of STEM Democratization," *Teachers College Record* 122, no. 2 (2020), 18.

16. Cipollone, Stich, and Weis, "STEM for All," 7.

17. Catherine Riegle-Crumb, "The Path Through Math: Course Sequences and Academic Performance at the Intersection of Race-Ethnicity and Gender," *American Journal of Education* 113, no. 1 (2006): 101–22.

18. David T. Burkam and Valerie E. Lee, "Mathematics, Foreign Language, and Science Coursetaking and the NELS: 88 Transcript Data" (working paper No. 2003-01, National Center for Education Statistics, Washington, DC, 2003); Xin Ma and Laureen J. McIntyre, "Exploring Differential Effects of Mathematics Courses on Mathematics Achievement," *Canadian Journal of Education/Revue Canadienne de L'éducation* (2005): 827–52; Catherine Riegle-Crumb, "The Path Through Math."

19. Sharon J. Lynch et al., "Inclusive STEM-Focused High Schools: STEM Education Policy and Opportunity Structures" (paper presented at the annual conference of the National Association for Research in Science Teaching (NARST), Rio Grande, Puerto Rico, April 6–9, 2013); Sharon J. Lynch et al., "Understanding Inclusive STEM High Schools as Opportunity Structures for Underrepresented Students: Critical Components," *Journal of Research in Science Teaching* 55, no. 5 (2018): 712–48.

CHAPTER 4

1. Christopher D. Schmidt, Gail B. Hardinge, and Laurie J. Rokutani, "Expanding the School Counselor Repertoire through STEM-Focused Career Development," *The Career Development Quarterly* 60, no. 1 (2012): 25–35, https://doi.org/10.1002/j.2161-0045.2012.00003.

2. Schmidt, Hardinge, and Rokutani, "Expanding the School Counselor Repertoire," 26.

3. The college admissions process in the United States has become increasingly complex. With an eye toward maintaining class privilege, highly economically capitalized families increasingly expend energy and funds to position their children for entrance to particularly located postsecondary institutions. (See Lois Weis, Kristin Cipollone, and Heather Jenkins, *Class Warfare* [Chicago: University of Chicago Press, 2014].) The degree to

which privileged parents consciously work to position their children for college admissions and beyond (see Laura Hamilton, *Parenting to a Degree*, [Chicago: University of Chicago Press, 2016]) contributes to an intensifying arc of inequality in the United States, putting children of less highly capitalized families further and further behind compared to their more privileged counterparts. Under these circumstances, high school counselors can play a critical role in positioning students for post-high school education and engaging the college admissions process.

4. Sharon J. Lynch et al., "A Policy-Relevant Instrumental Case Study of an Inclusive STEM-Focused High School: Manor New Tech High," *International Journal of Education in Mathematics, Science and Technology* 5, no. 1 (2017): 1–20, https://eric.ed.gov/?id=EJ1124943.

5. Schmidt, Hardinge, and Rokutani, "Expanding the School Counselor Repertoire," 27.

6. Schmidt, Hardinge, and Rokutani, "Expanding the School Counselor Repertoire," 28–30.

7. Some of the data included here from the Buffalo schools were originally published in Andrea B. Nikischer, Lois Weis, and Rachel Dominguez, "Differential Access to High School Counseling, Postsecondary Destinations, and STEM Careers," *Teachers College Record* 118, no. 11 (2016): n11. These data are based on Andrea Nikischer's dissertation, "Social Class and the STEM Career Pipeline: An Ethnographic Investigation of Opportunity Structures in a High-Poverty Versus Affluent High School" (Order No. 3598726, State University of New York at Buffalo, 2013, https://www-proquest-com.gate.lib.buffalo.edu/dissertations-theses/social-class-stem-career-pipeline-ethnographic/docview/1459753763/se-2?accountid=14169) and include data for the account of Forestview High School below. Andrea Nikischer was a graduate assistant on this project and completed her dissertation under the direction of Lois Weis. Rachel Dominguez was a graduate assistant and a postdoctoral associate on this project and completed her dissertation under the direction of Lois Weis.

8. Student Support Teams are defined as "teams of school staff dedicated to identifying and supporting students who exhibit academic or behavioral problems by providing early systematic assistance to students and to connect them to appropriate interventions and supports." US Department of Education, "Issue Brief: Student Support Teams," last modified January 2017, https://www2.ed.gov/rschstat/eval/high-school/student-support-teams.pdf.

9. This situation in which teachers did not know final course assignments or had course assignments changed one month into the school year characterized several of our Buffalo schools.

10. Some data about Denver in this section come from Sarah Ohle Leibrandt's dissertation, "College-Going Capital: Understanding the Impact of College Readiness Policies on Schools and Students" (University of Colorado at Boulder, Ann Arbor, 2016; *ProQuest,* https://www-proquest-com.gate.lib .buffalo.edu/dissertations-theses/college-going-capital-understanding -impact/docview/1793670299/se-2?accountid=14169). Leibrandt was a graduate student in Educational Foundations, Policy, and Practice at CU-Boulder when she worked with Eisenhart on parts of the study reported in this book.

11. College-linking programs are defined as "school resource structures and norms for facilitating college transitions" in Lori Diane Hill, "School Strategies and the 'College-Linking' Process: Reconsidering the Effects of High Schools on College Enrollment," *Sociology of Education* 81, no. 1 (2008): 53–76, https://doi.org/10.1177/003804070808100103.

12. Although not a college-linking program in the same sense, programs like Buffalo Prep and others that begin working with academically talented students in middle school and throughout high school can provide similar activities with regard to the college preparation process. Students in Prep and similar programs receive important help with college applications, scholarship searches, and test preparation as well as with "soft skills" that help to ensure success as they move to the postsecondary sector.

13. Schmidt, Hardinge, and Rokutani, "Expanding the School Counselor Repertoire," 26.

14. "Education Professionals," College Board, https://professionals.college board.org/.

CHAPTER 5

1. A. Susan Jurow, "Shifting Engagements in Figured Worlds: Middle School Mathematics Students' Participation in an Architectural Design Project," *The Journal of the Learning Sciences* 14, no. 1 (2005): 35–67, https://doi.org /10.1207/s15327809jls1401_3.

2. Beth Rubin, "Learner Identity Amid Figured Worlds: Constructing (In) Competence at an Urban High School," *Urban Review* 39, no. 2 (2007): 240, https://doi.org/10.1007/s11256-007-0044-z.

3. Rubin, "Learner Identity," 222.

4. Dorothy Holland et al., *Identity and Agency in Cultural Worlds* (Cambridge, MA: Harvard University Press, 1998).

5. Holland et al., *Identity and Agency,* 52.

6. Holland et al., *Identity and Agency,* 52.

7. Luis Urrieta, "Identity Production in Figured Worlds: How Some Mexican Americans Become Chicana/o Activist Educators," *The Urban Review* 39, no. 2 (2007): 117–44, https://doi.org/10.1007/s11256-007-0050-1.

8. Urrieta, "Identity Production," 121.

9. Jo Boaler, "Mathematics from Another World: Traditional Communities and the Alienation of Learners," *The Journal of Mathematical Behavior* 18, no. 4 (2000): 379–97, https://doi.org/10.1016/S0732-3123(00)00026-2.

10. Rubin, "Learner Identity," 224.

11. Rubin, "Learner Identity," 224.

12. Katherine Wade-Jaimes and Renee Schwartz, "I Don't Think It's Science: African American Girls and the Figured World of School Science," *Journal of Research in Science Teaching* 56, no. 6 (2019): 679–706, https://doi.org /10.1002/tea.21521. It is important to underscore the contextual nature of notions of figured worlds, and particularly in this instance, what comprises a student who is good at math or science in any given context. The distributed and embodied notion that being good in math or science means being quiet, polite, and simply engaging in a practice of imitation does not necessarily characterize notions of being a good student in high schools that serve more highly capitalized students, particularly those in advanced math and science courses. Research in more privileged high schools reveals far deeper engagement with subject matter across the board, wherein notions of being "good" in math or science go beyond simple imitation and replication. In some schools that serve a more highly capitalized population, for example, someone who is considered "good at math" might be developing a new draft mathematics textbook with a teacher or challenging taken-for-granted mathematical understandings. The point is not that everyone can or should engage in these activities, but that what being "good at math" means emerges in relation to what comprises legitimate knowledge in any given context and the extent to which students are encouraged to reflect upon and challenge what is taken for granted. See also Rubén Gaztambide-Fernández, *The Best of the Best: Becoming Elite at an American Boarding School* [Cambridge, MA: Harvard University Press, 2009; Lois Weis, Kristin Cipollone, and Heather Jenkins, *Class Warfare: Class, Race and College Admissions in Top-Tier Secondary Schools* (Chicago: University of Chicago Press, 2014); and Shamus Rahman Khan, *Privilege* (Princeton, NJ: Princeton University Press, 2010). Jean Anyon also stressed this point in her early work on differential knowledge in the elementary schools in "Social Class and School Knowledge," *Curriculum Inquiry* 11, no. 1 (1981): 3–42, https://doi.org/10.1080/03626784 .1981.11075236.

13. Wade-Jaimes and Schwartz, "I Don't Think It's Science," 700.

14. Boaler, "Mathematics from Another World," 392.

15. Note that this is how we investigated figured worlds, but it's not the only way to investigate them. Rubin ("Learner Identity") and Wade-Jaimes and Schwartz ("I Don't Think It's Science") take a more robust approach (based on more observational detail than we had).

16. Portions of this section were originally published in Margaret Eisenhart and Carrie D. Allen, "Hollowed Out: Meaning and Authoring of High School Math and Science Identities in the Context of Neoliberal Reform," *Mind, Culture, and Activity* 23, no. 3 (2006): 188–98, doi: 10.1080/10749039.2016 .1188962. Reprinted with permission from the publisher (Taylor & Francis, Ltd). The definition of school as a place to exchange obedience and work for knowledge and teachers' guidance is from Paul Willis, *Learning to Labour: How Working Class Kids Get Working Class Jobs* (London: Saxon House, 1977).

17. For some positive examples, see Angela Calabrese Barton et al., "Crafting a Future in Science: Tracing Middle School Girls' Identity Work over Time and Space," *American Educational Research Journal* 50, no. 1 (2013): 37–75, https://doi.org/10.3102/0002831212458142; Heidi B. Carlone, Sue Kimmel, and Christina Tschida, "A Rural Math, Science, and Technology Elementary School Tangled Up in Global Networks of Practice," *Cultural Studies of Science Education* 5, no. 2 (2010): 447–76, https://doi.org/10.1007 /s11422-009-9233-2; Heidi B. Carlone, Catherine M. Scott, and Cassi Lowder, "Becoming (Less) Scientific: A Longitudinal Study of Students' Identity Work from Elementary to Middle School Science," *Journal of Research in Science Teaching* 51, no. 7 (2014): 836–69, https://doi.org/10.1002 /tea.21150; Margaret Eisenhart and Carrie D. Allen, "Addressing Underrepresentation of Young Women of Color in Engineering and Computing Through the Lens of Sociocultural Theory," *Cultural Studies of Science Education* 15, no. 3 (2020): 793–824, https://doi.org/10.1007/s11422-020 -09976-6; Jurow, "Shifting Engagements in Figured Worlds."

18. Portions of the work on figured worlds in Buffalo were previously published in Kristin Cipollone, Amy E. Stich, and Lois Weis, "STEM for All: Student Identities and the Paradox of STEM Democratization," *Teachers College Record* 122, no. 2 (2020). *Teachers College Record*, unlike select other journals, does not necessitate formal permission to use portions of authors' published work.

19. In New York State, Adequate Yearly Progress (AYP) is measured by annual state assessments, Regents examination scores, and graduation rates.

20. Weis, Cipollone, and Jenkins, *Class Warfare*.

21. *Hannah Montana* is a television show that featured pop singer Miley Cyrus. Francis's embarrassment comes from the fact that this is a children's show and is not perceived to be a legitimate source of information about colleges.

CHAPTER 6

1. Thomas A. DiPrete and Gregory M. Eirich, "Cumulative Advantage as a Mechanism for Inequality: A Review of Theoretical and Empirical Developments," *Annual Review of Sociology* 32 (2006): 271–97; Michelle Lee Maroto, "Pathways into Bankruptcy: Accumulating Disadvantage and the Consequences of Adverse Life Events," *Sociological Inquiry* 85, no. 2 (2015): 183–216.
2. Maroto, "Pathways into Bankruptcy," 184.
3. This chapter benefited from detailed analyses of the qualitative and quantitative data conducted by Rachel Dominguez, Seong Won Han, and Chungseo Kang.
4. We obtained additional information about two students in 2021, when they contacted our research team to inform us of their current status, and we include these data in the analyses.
5. Catherine Riegle-Crumb and Eric Grodsky, "Racial-Ethnic Differences at the Intersection of Math Course-Taking and Achievement," *Sociology of Education* 83, no. 3 (2010): 248–70; Awilda Rodriguez and Esmeralda Hernandez-Hamed, "Understanding Unfulfilled AP Potential Across the Participation Pipeline by Race and Income," *Teachers College Record* 122, no. 9 (2020): n9; Awilda Rodriguez and Keon M. McGuire, "More Classes, More Access? Understanding the Effects of Course Offerings on Black-White Gaps in Advanced Placement Course-Taking," *The Review of Higher Education* 42, no. 2 (2019): 641–79.
6. Advanced Placement and International Baccalaureate courses taken in high school offer the possibility of college course credit, while Regents and honors high school courses do not.
7. https://www2.ed.gov/about/offices/list/ocr/docs/stem-course-taking.pdf.
8. It is important to note the time frame for the in-school portion of the study was in the early 2010s. In 2015, a new superintendent was hired in Buffalo and has remained in the position for the past six years. His contract was recently renewed for an additional two years. This has led to more stability in the system, with consistent leadership and much less turnover. In other words, the reform churn in Buffalo is less tumultuous now. This does not, however, take away from the outcomes experienced by the Buffalo students in this sample. The inconsistency they

experienced has had long-term consequences on their STEM trajectories (or lack thereof).

9. These selectivity categories are from *Barron's Profiles of American Colleges: 2007* (Hauupauge, NY: Barron's Educational Series), 252. We used Barron's Profiles of American College: 2013 to categorize the colleges attended by our students who graduated from high school in 2013.

10. Adam Gamoran, "American Schooling and Educational Inequality: A Forecast for the 21st Century," *Sociology of Education* (2001): 135–53; Samuel R. Lucas, "Effectively Maintained Inequality: Education Transitions, Track Mobility, and Social Background Effects," *American Journal of Sociology* 106, no. 6 (2001): 1642–90.

CHAPTER 7

1. Joseph L. Polman and Diane Miller, "Changing Stories: Trajectories of Identification Among African American Youth in a Science Outreach Apprenticeship," *American Educational Research Journal* 47, no. 4 (2010): 879–918, doi.org/10.3102/0002831210367513; Stanton Wortham, *Learning Identity: The Joint Emergence of Social Identification and Academic Learning* (Cambridge, UK: Cambridge University Press, 2006).

2. This section was originally published in Margaret Eisenhart and Carrie D. Allen, "Hollowed Out: Meaning and Authoring of High School Math and Science Identities in the Context of Neoliberal Reform," *Mind, Culture, and Activity* 23, no. 3 (2016): 188–98. Reprinted with permission from the publisher (Taylor & Francis Ltd.).

3. Ebony Omotola McGee, *Black, Brown, Bruised: How Racialized STEM Education Stifles Innovation* (Cambridge, MA: Harvard Education Press, 2021), 66–74. See also her references for this point in footnote 26, p. 167.

4. McGee, *Black, Brown, Bruised*, 68, 71.

5. Melanie LaForce et al., "Revisiting Race and Gender Differences in STEM: Can Inclusive STEM High Schools Reduce Gaps?," *European Journal of STEM Education* 4, no. 1 (2019): 8.

6. By "verified," we mean that we have evidence that these students graduated with a college major in STEM as of 2019.

7. For example, see Lois Weis, Kristin Cipollone, and Heather Jenkins, *Class Warfare* (Chicago: University of Chicago Press, 2014); Shamus Rahman Shan, *Privilege: The Making of an Adolescent Elite at St. Paul's School* (Princeton, NJ: Princeton University Press, 2021); Adam Howard, *Learning Privilege: Lessons of Power and Identity in Affluent Schooling* (Oxford, UK: Routledge, 2013).

8. McGee, *Black, Brown, Bruised: How Racialized STEM Education Stifles Innovation.*

9. The first letter of the pseydonyms used in this chapter indicate the high school attended by these students; that is, names beginning with *C* are Capital students, names beginning with *A* are from Chavez, names beginning with *P* are from Pella, and names beginning with *S* are from Southside. This convention makes it easier to situate each student in their school when reading about them.

10. For some of these students, like Padma, English was not her first language, but native English-speaking students made similar comments about language arts.

11. AVID is a privately funded program to prepare low-income and underserved students for college admission and success. It was available and utilized by students in the Denver schools in our study. See chapter 4.

12. Talent Search is a federally funded program to assist youth from disadvantaged backgrounds to finish high school and prepare for college. It was also available and utilized by students in the Denver schools in our study.

13. We should note here that the boys who participated in our Denver study were, for the most part, interviewed and observed by male researchers.

14. See www.onet.org, developed by the Colorado Department of Education and available on the *College in Colorado* website that teachers, counselors, students, and parents in our study had access to but rarely used.

15. See also Julia C. Duncheon, "'You Have to Be Able to Adjust Your Own Self': Latinx Students' Transitions into College from a Low-Performing Urban High School," *Journal of Latinos and Education* 17, no. 4 (2018): 358–372. She describes a similar pattern of seeking out help among Latinx women who struggle to pursue STEM in college.

CHAPTER 8

1. For a relatively recent review and update, see Prudence Carter and Kevin Welner, *Closing the Opportunity Gap* (Oxford, UK: Oxford University Press, 2013).

2. Adam Gamoran, "American Schooling and Educational Inequality: A Forecast for the 21st Century," *Sociology of Education* (2001): 135–53; Sean Reardon, "The Widening Academic Achievement Gap Between the Rich and the Poor: New Evidence and Possible Explanations," in *Whither Opportunity? Rising Inequality, Schools, and Children's Life Chances*, eds. Greg J. Duncan & Robert J. Murnane (New York: Russell Sage Foundation, 2011), 91–116.

3. Jaekyung Lee, *The Anatomy of Achievement Gaps: Why and How American Education Is Losing (But Can Still Win) the War on Underachievement* (Oxford, UK: Oxford University Press, 2016), 4.

4. National Research Council. Successful K–12 STEM Education: Identifying Effective Approaches in Science, Technology, Engineering, and Mathematics. (Washington, DC: Government Printing Office, 2011); Roy D. Pea and Allan Collins, "Learning How to Do Science Education: Four Waves of Reform," *Designing Coherent Science Education* 3 (2008): 12; Joan Ferrini-Mundy, "Driven by Diversity," *Science* 340, no. 6130 (2013): 278.

5. It is also worthwhile to note that the Buffalo school system experienced very regular turnover of superintendents over the lifespan of this project, with six different individuals serving as superintendent from 2010 to 2015. From 2015 to present (2021), one superintendent has remained at the helm.

6. Kristin Cipollone and Amy E. Stich, "Shadow Capital: The Democratization of College Preparatory Education," *Sociology of Education* 90, no. 4 (2017): 333–54, 333.

7. Thomas A. DiPrete and Gregory M. Eirich, "Cumulative Advantage as a Mechanism for Inequality: A Review of Theoretical and Empirical Developments," *Annual Review of Sociology* 32 (2006): 272.

8. Michelle Lee Maroto, "Pathways into Bankruptcy: Accumulating Disadvantage and the Consequences of Adverse Life Events," *Sociological Inquiry* 85, no. 2 (2015): 183–216.

9. Samuel R. Lucas, "Effectively Maintained Inequality: Education Transitions, Track Mobility, and Social Background Effects," *American Journal of Sociology* 106, no. 6 (2001): 1642–90.

10. Jason Fletcher and Marta Tienda, "Race and Ethnic Differences in College Achievement: Does High School Attended Matter?," *The Annals of the American Academy of Political and Social Science* 627, no. 1 (2010): 144–66.

11. Erika C. Bullock, "Only STEM Can Save Us? Examining Race, Place, and STEM Education as Property," *Educational Studies* 53, no. 6 (2017): 628–41, 628.

12. The term "booster shot" was first used in this regard by Andrea Nikischer in her dissertation linked to this project, "Social Class and the STEM Career Pipeline: An Ethnographic Investigation of Opportunity Structures in a High-Poverty Versus Affluent High School," Order No. 3598726, State University of New York at Buffalo, 2013, https://www-proquest-com.gate .lib.buffalo.edu/dissertations-theses/social-class-stem-career-pipeline -ethnographic/docview/1459753763/se-2?accountid=14169.

13. This idea of "boot camps" for math in particular was suggested to our research team by Amanda Simmons, a highly regarded high school math teacher who has taught rigorous math courses at a range of prestigious educational institutions in the nation.

14. Lois Weis, Kristin Cipollone, and Heather Jenkins, *Class Warfare* (Chicago: University of Chicago Press, 2014).

15. Sharon J. Lynch et al., "Understanding Inclusive STEM High Schools as Opportunity Structures for Underrepresented Students: Critical Components," *Journal of Research in Science Teaching* 55, no. 5 (2018): 712–48.

16. A related issue here is what is meant by "good jobs" in STEM fields. There is a persistent assumption in much of the STEM literature that "good jobs" are those in the most elite STEM professions; that is, academic and research positions. We think it is important to emphasize that although diverse young people may not (yet) be well represented in the most elite STEM positions, they, including many of the focal students in our study, are contributing in large numbers to critical STEM-related needs and finding lucrative and rewarding jobs in these areas. They are already part of what Bottia et al. call the "professional STEM labor force," and in so being, they are responding to "national and global crises in health and medicine, national security, the economy, and climate" and enhancing their own "chances for economic and social mobility" (Martha Cecilia Bottia et al., "Factors Associated with College STEM Participation of Racially Minoritized Students: A Synthesis of Research," *Review of Educational Research* [2021]: 00346543211012751, 26).

APPENDIX

1. Erica Frankenberg and Genevieve Siegel-Hawley, "Choice Without Equity: Charter School Segregation and the Need for Civil Rights Standards," *The Education Digest* 76, no. 5 (2011): 44, http://epaa.asu.edu/ojs/article/view/779.

2. David Stern, Charles Dayton, and Marilyn Raby, "Career Academies: A Proven Strategy to Prepare High School Students for College and Careers," *Career Academy Support Network* (2010), ERIC ED524061.

3. Lois Weis, Kristin Cipollone, and Heather Jenkins, *Class Warfare* (Chicago: University of Chicago Press, 2014).

4. Data are found in Thomas D. Snyder, Christobal De Brey, and Sally A. Dillow, "Digest of Education Statistics 2015, NCES 2016-014," *National Center for Education Statistics* (2016), https://nces-ed-gov.gate.lib.buffalo.edu/pubs2016/2016014.pdf.

5. Snyder, De Brey, and Dillow, "Digest of Education Statistics," 956.

6. Snyder, De Brey, and Dillow, "Digest of Education Statistics," 185.

7. Matthew B. Miles, A. Michael Huberman, and Johnny Saldaña, *Qualitative Data Analysis: A Methods Sourcebook* (Los Angeles: SAGE Publications, 2014).

8. We obtained additional information about two students in 2021, when they contacted our research team to inform us of their current status, and we include these data in the analyses.

9. Barbara Schneider, *Forming Better STEM Career Trajectories: Sustaining and Scaling-Up College Access Programs,* National Science Foundation, DRL #1316702.

10. For a meta-analysis of school turnaround models, see Christopher Redding and Tuan D. Nguyen, "The Relationship Between School Turnaround and Student Outcomes: A Meta-Analysis," *Educational Evaluation and Policy Analysis* 42, no. 4 (2020): 493–519.

ACKNOWLEDGMENTS

From its earliest conception to these last few sentences, we have been working on this project since 2009. Not surprisingly, there are a large number of individuals and groups who contributed to our work. It is hard to know where to begin. We thank the district- and building-level administrators who facilitated access to the sites and agreed to be interviewed. We thank the teachers, counselors, and school-based support staff who participated in our ethnographic investigation. These individuals welcomed our research teams and facilitated our work over the course of three years. Although they must remain nameless for reasons of confidentiality, we very much appreciate all their assistance over the sustained period of the project. Although the promises of STEM school reform were not wholly fulfilled in either city, school district- and building-level personnel worked hard, often in challenging situations, to serve their low-income and underrepresented students.

We also thank all the focal students, their parents, and their guardians for speaking with us over the course of the investigation, and especially those focal students with whom we reconnected after they graduated from high school. Although the STEM reform effort did not result in everything they and their families had hoped for, these students kept moving forward, striving for a better life for themselves and their immediate and extended families. We have the highest respect for their efforts and their accomplishments.

During the long period of data collection, analysis, and writing, we worked with a large number of graduate students and postdoctoral associates. The care with which our graduate students and postdoctoral associates entered and sustained key relationships in the field was truly remarkable, as was their dedication to the research process and their forbearance with the many twists and turns of a large-scale research project involving so many people. In particular, we thank Carrie Allen, Margaret Burns, Jarrod Hanson, Sarah Ohle Leibrandt, Ruth Lopez, Joshua Prudhomme, Enrique Suarez, Michael Suarez, Michael Turner, and Liliana Vasquez who worked as school ethnographers in Denver. In Buffalo, we particularly thank Kristin Cipollone, Andrea Nikischer, and Amy Stich who worked as school ethnographers in Buffalo, and whose own subsequent writing and publications contributed to the argument presented in this volume. In Denver, we also thank Joe Harding, Lisa Schwartz, Kathryn Wiley, and Terri Wilson who contributed to data management and analysis, and in Lisa's case, also conducted follow-up interviews. Anne Bliss contributed valuable editing assistance. In Buffalo, Ashley Aldridge, Erica Boyce, Nancy Campos, Rachel Dominguez, Ana Luisa Munoz Garcia, Chelsie Hinkley, Melissa Hubbard, Khristian King, Miao Li, Marissa Pytlak, Maiyuwai Reeves, and Teya Yu helped to coordinate transcription and analysis of the data; and Kathryn Goldbach organized and categorized our extensive online data files. Rachel Dominguez, Darlene Garcia Torres, Katie Reeb-Reascos, Carolina Rojas Pion, Jennifer Serniuk, and Michelle Wing conducted follow-up interviews in Buffalo and Denver. Shuyi Zhao assisted Rachel Dominguez with citations for this manuscript. Postdoctoral Associates Chungseo Kang and Hyunmyung Jo conducted descriptive quantitative analysis and reviews of relevant literature. Postdoctoral Associate Rachel Dominguez conducted careful analysis of all post-high school outcome data and functioned as overall project coordinator at the University at Buffalo during the latter years of the project. She also assisted in the production of this manuscript, masterfully holding all the component parts together. We are deeply grateful to all these individuals.

We were very fortunate to be generously funded by the National Science Foundation (Awards DRL 1007964 to Margaret Eisenhart and DRL 1008215 to Lois Weis). We thank our NSF Program Officers Myles Boylan and the late Karen King, as well as Finbarr Sloane and the late Janice Earle at NSF, who supported our work. We were also fortunate to have strong support and critical input from our NSF grant Advisory Board members. They included Frank Bright, SUNY Distinguished Professor of Chemistry and A. Conger Goodyear Chair at University at Buffalo; Jacqueline Eccles, Distinguished Professor of Education at the University of California, Irvine; Joseph Gardella, Professor and Larkin Chair of Chemistry at University at Buffalo; E. Bruce Pittman, Associate Dean for Research and Sponsored Programs and Professor of Mathematics at University at Buffalo; and Esther Takeuchi, SUNY Distinguished Professor of Chemical and Biological Engineering at University at Buffalo. The input of Advisory Board members was critical to the short- and long-term success of this project. Data analyzed as part of a subsequent NSF grant to Lois Weis and Seong Won Han (DGE #1660402) informed elements of the analysis and argument presented in this volume, particularly with respect to math-taking patterns. We are grateful to NSF and particularly Seong Won Han, a valued colleague at the University at Buffalo, for her dedication to this project. We additionally thank Jolene Jesse, our NSF Program Officer, for the subsequent grant, and additional Advisory Board members: Hong Luo, Professor of Physics at University at Buffalo; Barbara Means, Executive Director of Digital Promise; Laura Perna, Centennial Presidential Professor of Education and co-founder of the Alliance for Higher Education and Democracy at the University of Pennsylvania; and Barbara Schneider, John A. Hannah Chair University Distinguished Professor in the College of Education and Department of Sociology at Michigan State University. We are deeply grateful to NSF, our program officers, and all Advisory Board members for their continued support of our work.

We have also been fortunate to present numerous papers at national and international conferences and have benefited enormously from the comments of other panelists and respondents. We thank Angela Calabrese Barton, Professor, Educational Studies Department, University of Michigan; Jeanne Century, Director of Outlier Research & Evaluation at the Chicago STEM Education Program at the University of Chicago; Jacquelynne Eccles, Distinguished Professor of Education, University of California, Irvine; Adam Gamoran, President, WT Grant Foundation; Anthony Eamonn E. Kelly, NSF-EHR Senior Advisor and current Associate Dean for Research, College of Education and Human

Development, George Mason University; Sharon Lynch, Research Professor at the George Washington Institute for Public Policy and Professor Emerita in the Graduate School of Education and Human Development at the George Washington University; Patricia McDonough, Professor, Department of Education, University of California, Los Angeles; Barbara Means, Executive Director of Digital Promise; Na'ilah Suad Nasir, President, The Spencer Foundation; Beth Rubin, Professor and Chair of Educational Theory, Policy and Administration at Rutgers University; and Rena Subotnik, Director, Psychology in Schools and Education, Education Directorate, American Psychological Association.

Numerous colleagues and friends aided us throughout the research and writing process. Friend to both of us, Hilda Borko, of Stanford University, deserves special thanks. She realized before we did that each of us had similar ideas for a next research project, and she encouraged us to collaborate. Wisely, we did. We also thank Deans Mary Gresham, Jaekyung Lee, and Suzanne Rosenblith, University at Buffalo, and Dean Lorrie Shepard, University of Colorado Boulder for their consistent support of our ongoing work, as well as colleagues Xiufeng Liu, Bill Penuel, Catherine Riegle-Crumb, Noemi Waight, and Randy Yerrick for their helpful insights along the way. Thanks also to Jayne Fargnoli, Editor in Chief, and Molly Grab, Editorial Assistant, of Harvard Education Press, who led us through the publication process. Our final thanks go to our husbands, Tereffe Asrat and Joe Harding, who make all things possible and have done so for many years.

ABOUT THE AUTHORS

MARGARET EISENHART is University Distinguished Professor Emerita of Educational Foundations and Research Methodology at the University of Colorado Boulder, USA. Trained as a cultural anthropologist, she specializes in educational anthropology and ethnographic research methods. Her research focuses on the social and cultural experiences of students in and outside of US schools and on applications of ethnographic methodology in educational research. She has written extensively on racial and gender dynamics and identities among elementary school students; gender imagery and relationships among college students; educational ethnography; and, most recently, student experiences of science, technology, engineering, and mathematics (STEM) in middle and high schools. From 1999 to 2013, she developed, directed, and conducted research on after-school programs in computing and engineering for high school girls of color who had little exposure to these subject areas. Her ethnographic, longitudinal, and action-oriented work has been generously funded by the National Science Foundation. Her most recent studies and writings (many with Lois Weis) examine underrepresented high school students' opportunities to learn STEM and the subsequent pathways they take to college and a career. Some of this research relies on text messaging and Facebook data, as well as more standard ethnographic techniques. She is the author or co-author of over 100 research articles and three books—*Educated in Romance: Women, Achievement and College Culture* (with Dorothy Holland; University of Chicago Press, 1990); *Designing Classroom Research* (with Hilda Borko; Allyn & Bacon, 1993); and *Women's Science: Learning and*

Succeeding from the Margins (with Elizabeth Finkel; University of Chicago Press, 1998). Her articles have appeared in numerous journals, including *Anthropology & Education Quarterly*; *Educational Researcher*; *American Educational Research Journal*; *Journal of the Learning Sciences* (with Carrie Allen; Best Paper Award, 2017); *Mind, Culture, and Activity*; *Journal of Research in Mathematics Education*; and *Journal of Research in Science Teaching*. She has served on the National Research Council and on the Board of the National Center for Women in Information Technology. She is a Fellow of the American Anthropological Association and of the American Educational Research Association. She is a member of the US National Academy of Education and has served on its board.

LOIS WEIS is State University of New York Distinguished Professor of Sociology of Education at the University at Buffalo. She has written extensively about the current predicament of White, African American, Latino/a, and Southeast Asian working class and poor youth and young adults, and the complex role gender and race/ethnicity play in their lives in light of contemporary dynamics associated with the global knowledge economy, new patterns of emigration, and the movement of cultural and economic capital across national boundaries. More recently, she, with Margaret Eisenhart, has turned her attention to the mechanisms through which low-income and historically underrepresented minoritized youth are denied access to opportunities for high-level STEM courses and associated college majors. Her books include *Class Warfare: Class, Race, and College Admissions in Top-Tier Secondary Schools* (with Kristin Cipollone and Heather Jenkins; University of Chicago Press, 2014); *Education and Social Class: Global Perspectives* (edited with Nadine Dolby; Routledge, 2012); *Class Reunion: The Remaking of the American White Working Class* (Routledge, 2004); and *Beyond Silenced Voices: Class, Race and Gender in United States Schools* (edited with Michelle Fine; SUNY Press, 2005), among others. Her articles have appeared in numerous journals, including *American Educational Research Journal*; *Journal of Higher Education*; *Harvard Educational Review*; *Teachers College Record*; *Journal of Research in Science Teaching*; *Signs: Journal of Women in Culture and Society*; *British Journal of Sociology of Education*; and *Anthropology and Education Quarterly*, among others. She is co-winner (with Michelle Fine) of the Outstanding Book Award for *Construction Sites: Excavating Race, Class and Gender Among Urban Youth* (Teachers College Record, 2000) from the Gustavus Myers Center for the Study of Bigotry and Human Rights in North America, as well as multiyear winner of the American Educational Studies Association's Critic's Choice Award, given for an outstanding book. Her research has been generously funded by the National Science Foundation, Carnegie Foundation, and Spencer Foundation, among others. She is past president of the American Educational Studies Association, past editor of the *American Educational Research Journal*, and founding and past editor of *Educational Policy*. She is an Honorary Fellow of the American Educational Research Association. She is a member of the US National Academy of Education and currently serves on its board.

INDEX

academic outcomes, 14–15, 99–128
  See also student outcomes
academy structure, 5–6, 24–31, 49,
  65, 159
accountability, 42–43, 49, 56–57,
  64, 159, 165
achievement gaps, 157–170
advanced courses, 80, 108–112, 141
  availability of, 89, 107–108,
    112–115, 164–166
  in eleventh and twelfth grades,
    143–149
  enrollment in, 166
  erosion of, 35–39, 43, 48–49, 50,
    65
  lack of, 66, 160
  selection of, 61
  struggles in, 143–149
Advanced Placement (AP) courses,
  8, 18, 23, 28, 34, 37, 43, 49, 61,
  86, 88–89, 107, 109–111, 114,
  115, 144–145
  See also advanced courses
Advancement Via Individual Determination (AVID), 69–70,
  145–146
advantage, cumulative, 99–100, 115,
  127–128, 160–163, 167–168
after-school programs, 18, 166, 168,
  207

ALEKS (Assessment and Learning
  in Knowledge Spaces) program,
  18
Algebra, 8, 22, 23, 34, 41, 85, 86
Algebra II/Trigonometry, 18, 22, 23,
  41, 42, 50, 84, 85, 86, 94, 109,
  112
anxiety, about college, 149
AP scores, 88
attainment gap, 157
AVID program. *See* Advancement
  Via Individual Determination
  (AVID)

Biopharmacy program, 8, 34,
  38–42, 48, 50, 59, 60
Black students, 1, 158, 165
  See also minoritized students
  advanced course offerings and,
    114
  in Buffalo, 4
Boaler, Jo, 79
Bourdieu, Pierre, 46
Buffalo
  advanced course offerings,
    110–115
  career outcomes in, 118–126
  demographics of, 6, 10
  erosion of STEM opportunities
    in, 33–51

Buffalo, *continued*
  figured worlds in, 85–97, 160
  focal students in, 10, 11
  guidance counseling in, 54–64,
    73–75
  influence of popular culture in,
    95–97
  lost opportunities in, 48–51
  low pass rates in, 42–45
  opportunity structures in, 20,
    22–23
  public support for STEM reform
    in, 33–34
  shadow capital in, 46–48, 51
  STEM education reform in, 3–4,
    6–9, 12–13, 33–35, 167–168
  STEM-focused schools in, 7–8,
    34–45
  student outcomes in, 14–15, 101,
    103–107, 117–118
Burdette, Tom, 38

Calculus, 19, 30, 37, 41, 42, 65, 84,
    85, 109, 112, 114, 115, 130, 131,
    165
capital
  accrued, 119, 125–126
  cultural, 46–48, 159
  definition of, 46
  economic, 46
  shadow, 46–49, 51, 97, 126, 128,
    153, 159, 160, 162
  social, 46
  STEM, 46–49, 51, 97, 126, 128,
    159, 162
"Capital effect," 118–119
career academies, 5, 49–50, 159, 172
Career and Technical Education
    (CTE) programs, 8, 19, 20,
    39–40, 42, 48, 50

career counseling, 13, 53, 61–64,
    73–75, 99, 159, 166
career outcomes, 5, 14–15, 99–128,
    118–126, 136–137
career plans, 61, 84–85
careers
  empty figured world for, 91–95
  popular culture and, 95–97
  STEM, 41, 50, 54, 84–85,
    118–126, 136–137, 160
Cipollone, Kristin, 47–48
classroom activities, 79
college acceptance rates, 73
college admissions, 93–94
  access to resources for, 67, 73
  AP scores and, 88
  high-level course offerings and,
    50
  lack of information about, 63, 73,
    91
  requirements for, 66
college applications, 55, 58, 63, 69,
    70–71, 74, 88, 146, 149
College Board, 8
college counseling, 13, 61–64,
    66–67, 73–75, 159
  outsourcing, 67–73, 99, 166
college enrollment, 31, 100, 103
college experiences, 153–154
college graduation outcomes,
    101–106, 115–118
College in Colorado, 71–73
college-linking programs, 64,
    68–71, 74, 95
college majors, 2, 71, 74, 101,
    120–122, 131–137, 149–153
college planning. *See* college
    counseling
college preparation, 29, 61–64, 68,
    91–95, 146

college readiness, 36
colleges and universities
    See also two-year institutions
    empty figured world for, 91–95
    partnerships with, 18, 34, 35, 99,
        166
    popular culture and, 95–97
college types, 115–118
community colleges, 25, 32, 68, 70,
    73, 148
competitiveness, of colleges,
    115–118
comprehensive high schools, 9
    guidance counseling at, 57–64
    opportunities in, vs.
        STEM-focused schools,
        19–24
    STEM offerings within, 2, 3, 13,
        19, 32, 41, 45, 48
core standards, 27
counseling. *See* guidance
    counseling
course content, erosion of, 41–42
course offerings, 20–23, 30–32
    See also math course offerings;
        science course offerings
    erosion of high-level, 13, 33–51,
        155–156, 159
    need for advanced, 164–166
course scaffolding, 48, 50, 61, 85,
    126, 127, 165, 182
course scheduling, 25, 29, 58–61,
    64–67, 74
cultural capital, 46–48, 159
cumulative advantage/disadvan-
    tage, 99–100, 115, 127–128,
    160–163, 167–168

data analysis, 176–178
data collection, 173–175

Denver
    advanced course offerings,
        110–115
    career outcomes in, 118–126
    demographics of, 4, 7
    erosion of STEM opportunities
        in, 49–50
    figured worlds in, 80–85, 97–98,
        160
    focal students in, 7, 10–11
    guidance counseling in, 13,
        64–75
    launch of reforms in, 17–30
    opportunity structure in, 18–30
    shadow capital in, 48
    STEM education reform in, 3–6,
        12–13, 17–30, 49, 165–166
    STEM-focused schools in, 5,
        17–30, 49
    STEM trajectories in, 129–156
    student outcomes in, 14–15,
        100–103, 105–107, 115–117
Denver School of Science and Tech-
    nology (DSST), 3
DiPrete, Thomas, 161
disadvantage, cumulative, 99–100,
    115, 127–128, 160–163,
    167–168
double class periods, 18–19, 32

economic capital, 46
educational bankruptcy, 162
educational inequities, 157
    See also cumulative advantage/
        disadvantage
educational opportunities, 167
    See also opportunity structures
educational outcomes, 14–15,
    99–128
    See also student outcomes

education reform. *See* STEM education reform
effectively maintained inequality,
126–128, 163
Eirich, Gregory, 161
eleventh grade, 143–149, 155
employment opportunities, 54
employment outcomes. *See* career
outcomes
ethnographic longitudinal studies,
164
exchange value, 47, 119
expectations, minimum, 86–91
extracurricular opportunities, 36
See also after-school programs

female students, 1, 138, 155, 160
figured worlds and, 79–80,
145–147
at inclusive STEM schools, 2
figured worlds, 77–98, 99
of "being good" in math or science, 86, 139–149, 155
in Buffalo, 85–97
of college and career, 91–95
definition of, 77
in Denver, 80–85
gender and, 79–80, 145–149
hollowed-out, 13–14, 80, 82, 99,
129, 133, 143, 146, 155–156,
160, 169
opportunity structures and,
97–98
order and ranking in, 78
of "passing," 86–91, 146–147,
160, 162
focal students, 3–4, 11–12, 161
in Buffalo, 10
in Denver, 7, 10–11
follow-up on, 158–159

outcomes for, 14–15, 99–128,
178–180
representativeness of, 175–176
selection of, 158
STEM identities of, 154–156
Forensic program, 8, 39–41, 42,
48–50, 59, 112

gender differences
in figured worlds, 79–80, 145–149
in student identities, 147–149, 155
girls, 1, 79–80, 138, 155, 160
"good" students, 78–91, 99,
131–133, 146, 154–156
See also high-achieving students
grades, 79, 81
graduation rates, 31, 40, 43, 45, 73
graduation requirements, 19–20,
27, 29, 43, 49, 66, 86, 159, 165
guidance counseling, 53–75
in Buffalo, 54–64
career counseling, 13, 53, 61–64,
73–75, 99, 159, 166
college counseling, 13, 61–64,
66–75, 99, 159, 166
course scheduling, 58–61, 64–67
in Denver, 64–73
lack of, for high-achieving students, 99
need for, 165
online programs, 71–73
outsourcing, 67–73
for STEM careers, 73–75
guidance counselors, 13
caseloads for, 65
important role of, 53, 54
limited attention to top students
by, 61–64
time crunch for, 53–54, 56–57,
67, 74, 159

training for, 54, 56
work of, 55–58

high-achieving students, 9, 97
    course scheduling and, 60
    "good" students, 78–91, 99,
        131–133, 146, 154–156
    grouping, 168–169
    identities of, 130–132
    lack of counseling for, 13, 61–64,
        66, 70–71, 73, 75, 99, 159
    meanings associated with being
        successful for, 13–14
    STEM trajectories of, 130–133
    success and, 82–84
higher education, 80
higher-order skills, 80
high-level course offerings. *See* ad-
    vanced courses
highly selective schools, 2
high-poverty areas, 46
high school graduation require-
    ments. *See* graduation
    requirements
high school guidance counseling.
    See guidance counseling
high school guidance counselors.
    See guidance counselors
high school models, for STEM edu-
    cation, 2
high school STEM course-taking,
    student outcomes and, 107–115
Holland, Dorothy, 77, 78
hollowed-out figured worlds, 13–14,
    80, 82, 99, 129, 133, 143, 146,
    155–156, 160, 169
honors courses, 21, 23, 28, 32, 36,
    37, 55, 84, 94, 107, 108, 112,
    143
    See also advanced courses

HOT (Health Occupations and
    Technology) program, 8,
    34–35, 40, 41, 48, 62
Hutchinson Technical High
    School, 3

IB courses, 108–111, 114
identity
    as "good" student, 85, 131–133
    school, 130–133
    "smart," 78
    STEM, 132–133
    student, 78, 80, 82, 84–85, 91,
        97–98, 143–144, 146,
        154–156
identity formation, 129
"imitation science" discourse,
    79–80
inclusive STEM-focused schools,
    157–158
    components of successful, 31
    diversity of, 2
    guidance counseling at, 53–54
    outcome data on, 2
    popularity of, 2
    research on, 2–3
    student outcomes and, 125
inequality
    effectively maintained, 126–128,
        163
    maintenance of, 126–128
    reproduction of, 99–100
    schools and, 162
institutional differentiation, 127,
    163
International Baccalaureate (IB)
    program, 18, 28, 65, 108–111,
    114
interpretive discourses, 13–14
intrinsic motivation, 133

job training, 41
Johns Hopkins Talent Development, 18

language arts, 140
Latino/a students, 1, 158
   advanced course offerings and, 114
   in Denver, 4
learning environments, 157
Lee, Jaekyung, 157
longitudinal studies, 164
low-income students, 1, 158
   boot camps for, 164–165, 166
   in Buffalo, 4, 11
   in Denver, 4, 10–11
   maintenance of inequality for, 126–128
   opportunities for, 167–168
   STEM-focused schools and, 30
   STEM-related outcomes for, 125
low-performing students, 31–32, 40, 64, 66, 67, 73
Lucas, Samuel, 127, 163
Lynch, Sharon, 31, 50–51

Maroto, Michelle, 161–162
material conditions, 77
math, 79
   double class periods for, 18–19
   figured worlds of success in, 77–98, 139–149, 160
   passion for, 132–133, 140–141
math course offerings, 20–23, 30–32, 107–108
   advanced courses, 108–115, 160
   erosion of, 35–43, 45, 48–50, 65
math courses, scaffolding of, 45, 50, 61, 85, 126, 127, 165, 182

math graduation requirements, 43
math proficiency, 45
McGee, Ebony Omotola, 132–133, 141
MESA (Mathematics, Engineering, Science Achievement) program, 18
minimum expectations, 86–91
minoritized students, 1, 11, 158
   advanced course offerings and, 114
   boot camps for, 164–165, 166
   high-achieving, 3–4
   maintenance of inequality for, 126–128
   opportunities for, 167–168
   STEM-focused schools and, 30
   STEM-related outcomes for, 125

Nasir, Na'ilah Suad, 167
Naviance, 71–73
No Child Left Behind, 56–57
nursing program, 8, 34–35

obedience, 81
occupational outcomes. *See* career outcomes
online programs, for college planning, 71–73, 74
opportunity structures
   in Denver, 18–30
   erosion of, 13, 33–51, 99, 126, 155–156, 159
   figured worlds and, 80, 97–98
   inequalities in, 157, 167–168
   lost, 48–51
   in STEM-focused vs. comprehensive high schools, 19–24
outcomes. *See* student outcomes

outsourcing
  to college-linking programs,
    68–71
  to online programs, 71–73

parent nights, 67
parents
  academy structure and, 29
  college resources and, 72
  course scheduling and, 59–60, 61
  in privileged communities, 167
  STEM education reform and, 3, 5,
    8, 9, 30
partnerships
  with colleges and universities, 34,
    35, 99, 166
  to enrich curricular, 18
passing, 86–91, 146–147, 160, 162
pass rates, low, 42–45
Persistently Lowest-Achieving (PLA)
  list, 40, 42–43, 45
popular culture, 95–97
postsecondary options, high-level
  course offerings and, 50
Precalculus, 19, 22, 38, 41, 42, 50,
    65, 81, 84, 85, 109, 112, 130,
    165
privileged communities, 167
programmatic erosion, 38–41, 50
project-based activities, 79

Race to the Top, 56–57
Regents examinations, 43, 86–91,
    108
remedial courses, 27, 39
research methodology, 171–183
Rubin, Beth, 79

sanctioned schools, 27
SAT scores, 63–64

scaffolding. *See* course scaffolding
school counselors. *See* guidance
  counselors
school identities, 130–133
school improvement plans, 64–65,
    73
schooling, figured worlds of success
  in, 77–98
school representativeness, 175–176
school site selection, 171–173
Schwartz, Renee, 79
science
  figured worlds of success in,
    77–98, 139–149, 160
  passion for, 132–133, 140–141
science course offerings, 20–23,
    30–32, 107–108
  advanced courses, 108–115, 160
  erosion of, 35–43, 45, 48–49
science graduation requirements,
    43
science proficiency, 45
serendipitous encounters, 152–153
shadow capital, 13, 46–49, 51, 97,
    126, 128, 153, 159, 160, 162
"smart" identity, 78
social capital, 46
social contexts, 78
social mobility, 46, 47, 159
socioeconomic status (SES), 10
staff turnover, 28, 30
standardized test scores, 2, 31, 32,
    42–45, 57, 64, 80, 86–91,
    157–158
standards-based learning, 29
state core standards, 27
STEM boot camps, 164–165, 166,
    168
STEM capital, 46–49, 51, 97, 126,
    128, 159, 162

STEM career counseling, 73–75
  See also career counseling
STEM careers, 41, 50, 84–85,
    136–137, 160
  college type and, 118–126
  guidance about, 54
  underrepresented groups in, 1
STEM courses
  See also advanced courses; math
      course offerings; science
      course offerings
  advanced, 108–109, 110–115
  in high school, and outcomes,
      107–115
STEM degrees, 105–107, 138, 160
STEM education
  exchange value of, 47
  high school models for, 2
  importance of, 1
  opportunity structure and,
      18–30
STEM education reform, 157, 161
  in Buffalo, 3–4, 6–9, 12–13,
      33–35, 167–168
  in Denver, 3–6, 12–13, 17–30,
      165–166
  introduction to, 1–15
  launching of, 17–32
  lessons learned for, 164–169
  public support for, 33–34, 50
  research on, 3–12
  results from, 50–51
  student outcomes and, 125, 169
  systemic, 157–160
STEM-focused schools
  academy structure at, 24–31
  appeal of, 30
  in Buffalo, 34–45
  components of successful, 31

  in Denver, 24–30, 49
  failures of, 30–32
  guidance counseling at, 54–75
  lost opportunities at, 48–51
  opportunities in, vs. comprehen-
      sive high schools, 19–24
  programmatic erosion at,
      38–41
  teachers at, 17–18, 34, 35
STEM identity, 132–133
STEM majors, 101, 103, 105, 106,
    115, 138
STEM opportunities, erosion of,
    33–51
STEM-related courses, 18
STEM trajectories, 129–156, 160
  advancement over time, 139–143
  choosing college major, 149–153
  college experiences, 153–154
  in eleventh and twelfth grades,
      143–149
  figured worlds and, 139–143
  of identification, 154–156
  serendipitous encounters and,
      152–153
Stich, Amy, 47–48
student achievement gaps,
    157–170
student identities, 78, 80, 82,
    84–85, 91, 97–98, 143–144,
    146, 154–156
student outcomes, 14–15, 158–159,
    178–180
  academic outcomes, 14–15,
      99–128
  in Buffalo, 14–15, 101, 103–107,
      117–118
  career outcomes, 5, 14–15,
      118–126, 136–137

college graduation outcomes,
101–106, 115–118
college types, 115–118
cumulative advantage/
disadvantage and,
99–100, 115
in Denver, 129–156
differences in, between cities,
161–163
for focal students, 99–128
high school STEM course-taking
and, 107–115
inequalities and, 126–128
overview of, 100–107
students
Black, 1, 4, 114, 158
comparisons of, 9–12
female. *see* female students
focal. *see* focal students
"good," 78–91, 99, 131–133, 146,
154–156
high-achieving. *see*
high-achieving students
interest in STEM by, 115
labeling of, 78
Latino/a, 1, 4, 114, 158
low-income. *see* low-income
students
low-performing, 31–32, 40, 64,
66, 67, 73
minoritized. *see* minoritized
students
tracking and SES, 10
student scheduling. *See* course
scheduling
subject matter interest, 140–141
success
figured worlds of, 77–98,
139–149, 160

as "passing," 86–91
in school, 80–83
stories of student, 132–139
systemic stratification, 127, 163

Talent Search, 69, 145–146
teacher assignment, 58–61
teachers, 142
staff turnover, 28, 30
at STEM-focused schools, 17–18,
26, 35
supportive, 144, 145–146, 155
training of, 17
Teach for Success, 18
technological developments, 54
television shows, 95–97
test scores, 2, 31, 32, 42–45, 57, 64,
80, 86–91, 88, 157–158
top-performing students. *See*
high-achieving students
traditional high schools. *See* comprehensive high schools
trajectories of identification,
129–156
Trigonometry. *See* Algebra II/
Trigonometry
twelfth grade, 143–149, 155
two-year institutions, 40, 41, 101,
103, 106, 107, 119, 123–125,
138
See also community colleges

underrepresented groups
career counseling for, 54
at inclusive STEM schools, 2
maintenance of inequality for,
126–128
in STEM-related fields, 1
Upward Bound, 69

Wade-James, Katherine, 79
Wilson, William Julius, 46
within-course content, erosion of,
    41–42

women
    See also female students
    underrepresentation of, in STEM
        fields, 1